ENCOUNTERS
Chinese Language and Culture

Character Writing Workbook 1

ENCOUNTERS
Chinese Language and Culture

Character Writing Workbook 1

漢字學習本
汉字学习本

John S. Montanaro
and
Rongzhen Li

Yale University

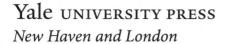
Yale UNIVERSITY PRESS
New Haven and London

Published with assistance from the Office of the President, Yale University.

Director of Digital Publishing: David Schiffman

Project Director: Mary Jane Peluso
Project Manager: Karen Hohner
Copy Editors: Joyce Ippolito and Yingjing Wang
Managing Editor: Jenya Weinreb
Designer and Compositor: Daniel Tschudi
Cover Designer: Wanda España/Wee Design Group
Production Controller: Maureen Noonan

Printed in the United States of America.

ISBN: 978-0-300-16170-0

This paper meets the requirements of ANSI / NISO Z39.48-1992 (Permanence of Paper).

10 9 8 7 6 5 4 3 2 1

Contents

Read This First!

Welcome to writing practice. This book is a companion to *Encounters* Student Book One, and it will help you learn the Chinese characters required for writing. Note that many other characters are presented in the Readings section of *Encounters,* but these are not practiced here. We practice here only those required for writing recall. Keep in mind that writing and learning go hand in hand, so practice in one leads to increased proficiency in the other. What's more, writing is also just plain fun. So give some time to developing a decent hand-writing. You'll be proud of yourself and of your Chinese. As you proceed, keep in mind the following tips.

Tactics and Strategies for Learning Characters

• Characters may seem, at first glance, an unorganized jumble of pen strokes, but, in fact, each character has one or more components that each contribute to the character. Although the total Chinese characters number in the tens of thousands, all characters are constructed from about 600 components in varying combinations. When you learn a character, it will be helpful if you pay close attention to components rather than look at the character as an isolated, haphazard collection of strokes. These sheets will help you in that effort.

• When you write a character, you do write it with individual strokes. Each stroke must be written in a prescribed sequence, such as left to right, top to bottom, and so on, and learning the proper order will be important to the rest of your study of Chinese. For example, if you see a character that you don't know, you will need to consult a Chinese dictionary. To do so successfully, you need to be able to count the strokes properly. Improper stroke order often leads to an incorrect stroke count, and missing a stroke here and there will lead you astray.

• Writing practice will help you understand the structure of Chinese characters, which helps retention. Writing will enable you to see the inner logic of characters, how they are built from two, three, or more components—which, again, will assist memory. Most Chinese characters are made up of one or more of these components, and these components are not haphazardly placed together but have definite, helpful-to-the-learner relationships. Learning the relationship of the parts leads to learning and better remembering the whole. Information contained on these sheets will help in that analysis. Here are a couple of examples of character formulation:

Combination of 'woman' and 'child' > 'good'

女 + 子 = 好 (*hǎo*)

Combination of 'man' and 'words' > 'trust'

人 + 言 = 信 (*xìn*)

(Note that components sometimes change shape when combined.)

• Practicing writing will deepen your appreciation of the beauty of China's written language. In this respect, no other language is its equal. Calligraphy, the art of fine writing, is perhaps the most celebrated of all China's arts. By practicing writing properly, you can not only have the practical benefits described above but also get closer to an appreciation of the elegance that is at the soul of Chinese writing and Chinese art.

• Finally, as one scholar of Chinese calligraphy has noted, many Chinese believe that the practice of writing prolongs one's life, sharpens one's senses, and improves one's overall health and well-being. To the Chinese, practicing writing characters is like a vitamin B-12 shot in the arm.

Questions Often Asked About Writing Chinese Characters

What shall I use to write characters? A brush? A pen?
While it would be wonderful to use the traditional Chinese writing implement, a brush, it's not practical in today's world. The writing brush or 毛笔 (*máobǐ*, ['hair' + 'pen']) is reserved for calligraphy or other forms of art. I advise using either a pencil, a fountain pen with a round tip, or a fine, black magic marker. Save the brush for the future.

What sort of practice paper should I use?
It is best to use paper marked off into squares, with each square large enough to contain a whole character. We provide a reproducible sample of such paper in this manual. Make enough copies to not only practice writing, but also to use when you're doing writing assignments, such as translations. Squared-off paper makes it easier to produce characters of uniform size and balance.

How shall I practice writing?
Here are some guidelines:

• First, trace the character in accordance with the correct stroke order, following the model provided for each character in this manual.

• As you practice, keep looking at the model, and compare your attempt with the model. If you make a mistake, start the character anew; don't erase your error.

• Practice about five characters per day, at least to begin with. Slow and steady wins the race. As you practice new characters, review earlier ones. For every five new ones, for example, review two or three old ones. Repetition is the key for all forms of foreign language learning: listening, speaking, reading, and writing.

• As you write the character, practice the pronunciation and tone of the character; each time you write, say it aloud. This will help concentration and keep your mind from wandering.

• Look for components in the character; finding and understanding them will help retention and help you see relationships and contrasts between similar characters. These sheets will help you in that effort.

- Save your practice sheets for later comparison. With practice, you will notice your progress.
  - Sit as upright as possible. This will help you to write properly.
  - Finally, as with all your language skills, daily practice is essential.

How much do I need to learn about each character?

On each character sheet we provide considerable information about each character. With your teacher's advice and guidance, you should learn as much as you can. As we have described above, you will at least need to learn how to write the character, its correct stroke order, its pronunciation and tone, and words associated with your lessons. Beyond that, we provide information about the radical, or 'meaning key,' which gives a generic clue to meaning, and also show you the shape of the character in earlier times—especially when the ancient form can act as a memory aid. We often also provide the phonetic of the character, which can give some information about the pronunciation of the character. The learning strategy is: the more you learn about a character, and the more associations you can make about the character, the better your chance to remember it.

The Eight Basic Strokes

The basic, individual strokes that make up all Chinese characters are not hard to master; putting them together to compose an elegant, balanced, harmonious character is the challenge for both Chinese native learners and foreign learners as well. The flourish here, the twist there, are all to a purpose, hardly accidental. Our purpose is not to turn you into a calligrapher but to help you achieve a decent handwriting that you'll be proud of.

In the Chinese writing tradition, eight basic strokes are recognized as fundamental and ever present. These eight basic strokes are traditionally associated with, appropriately, those that appear in the character 永 (*yǒng*, 'eternal').

The eight strokes are:

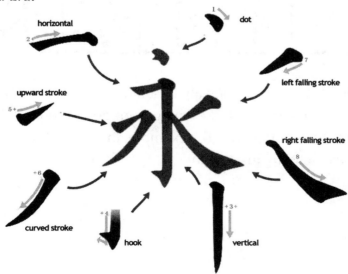

The stroke order is:

The direction of each stroke is:

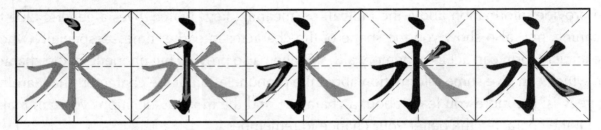

Exercise: Trace the following 永 (*yǒng*, 'eternal') and learn to write the basic strokes.

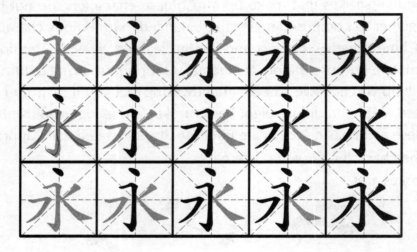

Note: Although the eight basic strokes are all present in 永, when 永 is commonly written in 'flowing' strokes, two or three of the strokes merge and do not require lifting the brush from the paper, making an actual total of five. For example, the second stroke, composed of three when written, is, in fact, actually just one.

Introductory Unit

Read over the list of characters below several times, reading over the characters first and then the pinyin pronunciation of each. When fluent, cover the pinyin and pronounce the character; be conscious of meaning and tone throughout. Make certain you have mastered the ten numbers and can recite them one through ten, ten through one, by even numbers, odd numbers, etc.

一	yī
二	èr
三	sān
四	sì
五	wǔ
六	liù
七	qī
八	bā
九	jiǔ
十	shí
火	huǒ
口	kǒu
木	mù
人	rén
山	shān
水	shuǐ

Chinese Characters: Pictographs

Chinese writing has ancient roots, dating back to thousands of years before the birth of Christ. The earliest specimens of Chinese writing that have come down to us consist of characters inscribed on bones of cattle, tortoise shells, and bronze vessels. You will see reproductions of these in the character sheets that follow in this book. Through thousands of years of continuous use, the characters have been formalized, stylized, or otherwise simplified, so what was once pure picture writing is no longer that at all. Characters that in their ancient form were curved and more flowing became, over the centuries, straighter, more upright, in shape. As you will soon appreciate more fully, however, the basic principles of character formulation—in other words, how a character is built—have not changed significantly over the centuries. The Chinese script remains a unique writing system that forms the basis of a modern, highly literate culture. Today, more people read and write Chinese than any other language in the world, and all of those people are using a writing system that is not based on an alphabet.

The study of the evolution of China's written script is a fascinating subject, but we can touch on only a few aspects here.

Ancient primitive pictures of concrete objects evolved over time into simple pictographs—pictures used to represent not only objects, but also ideas and concepts. And, even though the language has changed greatly since ancient times, many people still use the term 'pictograph' to describe the Chinese writing system. Characters with a clear, identifiable 'picture' within them are, for that reason, of greatest interest to learners, and perhaps easier to learn, but, regretfully, they form only a small part of the total amount of characters. You will learn, or have learned already, six of these 'pictographs.' 山 (*shān*, 'mountain'), 水 (*shuǐ*, 'water'), 人 (*rén*, 'person'), 口 (*kǒu*, 'mouth'), 木 (*mù*, 'tree'), and 火 (*huǒ*, 'fire'). Some also refer to this type of character as 'simplex,' given the simple structure, or as 'representational,' given the 'picture' qualities.

The Chinese early on developed a system for dividing characters into six categories (六書/六书, *liù shū*). We have simplified the six into three, the first of which, 'pictographs,' we present in this introduction, reserving the other two types for later lessons. On the next page are some more typically cited examples of pictographs with their earlier or representational forms detailed:

Ancient Form	Later Form	Modern Form	Meaning
		日	sun Day
		月	moon month
		水	water
		火	fire
		山	mountain
		人	person
		雨	rain
		土	soil
		口	mouth
		木	tree

rì

yuè

shǔi

hǔo

shan

In addition to concrete objects like those above, we also consider the following types of characters to be pictographic:

一	*yī*	one
二	*èr*	two
三	*sān*	three
上	*shàng*	above
下	*xià*	below

And, finally, we class combinations of single pictographs as belonging to the pictographic category of characters. For example: 木 means 'tree'; combine three trees together into 森 and you get the meaning 'forest.' 日 means 'sun' and 月 means 'moon,' both rather bright objects; combine them into 明 and you get the meaning 'bright.' Pretty cool how characters are built, right? You will learn more from the sheets about building characters as we go on. Fun in store!

A Useful Learning Strategy

We will tell you about strategies for learning and remembering characters. One of the most useful is to connect the 'picture' (the character itself or the 'picture' you create in your mind) with the meaning. Each time we detail information about a character in this manual, we will give you a memory link, a mnemonic device to key your memory. You will likely think of some yourself, and we encourage this. Any connection you can make between the character and meaning, no matter how fanciful, can be an invaluable memory aid. You're going to find that many of our memory clues are rather 'imaginative.' 'Purists' might argue (perhaps with good reason) with our memory aids, but keep in mind that our purpose is all about remembering. Any clue to memory is valuable. So imagine away!

Stroke Order: Basic Guidelines

There is usually a conventional sequence in which the strokes of Chinese characters are written, although there does exist some variation among Chinese writers. Diligent practice will soon fix the major principles in your mind. Here are some basic guidelines.

1. Left before right, as in 八 (*bā*, 'eight').

2. Top to bottom, as in 二 (*èr*, 'two').

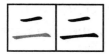

3. Horizontal line before vertical one, as in 十 (*shí*, 'ten').

4. Left-slanting line before an intersecting right-slanting line, as in 义 (*yì*, 'significance').

5. Central part before symmetrical sides, as in 小 (*xiǎo*, 'small').

6. Outside before inside, as in 同 (*tóng*, 'same').

7. If the 'enclosure' is complete on all four sides, the last stroke is the bottom one, as in 四 (*sì*, 'four').

8. If the character is framed from above, the frame is written first, as in 同 (*tóng*, 'same').

9. If the character is framed from the bottom, the frame is written last, as in 凶 (*xiōng*, 'ferocious').

These rules will not cover every situation, but they apply to the overwhelming majority of cases. Refer to them often and practice them frequently. Most or all of them will become automatic as you learn to write more and more characters.

A Guide to the Information on Character Sheets

- Boxes: Pronunciation of the character in pinyin, meaning of the character in English, common word or phrase using the character, ancient and later forms of the character, modern traditional form, and simplified form (if any).

jiàn	Ancient Form	Later Form	Modern Traditional Form	Modern Simplified Form
see; meet up with	罗	見	見	见
Zàijiàn!			再見!	再见!

- Information about the character, including radical, phonetic, memory aid, etc.

見/见 (*jiàn*) combines a large 目 (*mù*, 'eye') on top of an altered 人 (*rén*, 'person') and easily renders the meaning 'to see,' or the extended meaning 'to go to see; to meet up with.' Like many simplified characters, the modern simplified form derives from the common handwritten form. Many commonly used handwritten forms, popular for many years among the people, became official simplified characters, so the transition to simplified characters was a relatively easy task for native speakers of Chinese. Our task as second language learners is not so easy.

- Usage of the character in words, phrases, and sentences.

• 再見 Lynn!
• 明天 (*míngtiān*, 'tomorrow') 見.
• 一會兒 (*yí huìr*, 'little while') 見.
• 李老師 (*Lǐ Lǎoshī*, 'teacher') 再見!

• 再见 Lynn!
• 明天 (*míngtiān*, 'tomorrow') 见.
• 一会儿 (*yí huìr*, 'little while') 见.
• 李老师 (*Lǐ Lǎoshī*, 'teacher') 再见!

- Stroke-by-stroke guide to writing the character; squares for you to practice writing the character.

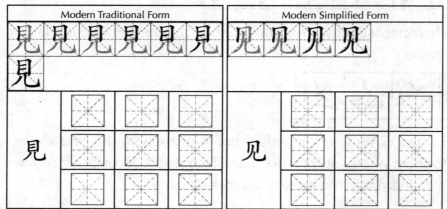

Copyright © 2012 by Yale University and China International Publishing Group

yī	The ancient form, later form, and modern form are all the same.
one, a/an (*1 stroke; left to right*)	一
èr	No change throughout history.
two (*2 strokes, top shorter than bottom*)	二
sān	No change throughout history.
three (*3 strokes; note sizes of individual strokes*)	三

The characters 一, 二, and 三 are all representational, with obvious meanings.

sì	Ancient Forms	Modern Form
four (*5 strokes; seal the box last*)	亖 𠚤	四

四 is, according to some, a pictograph of a four-sided square divided into 'four' parts. The four parallel lines version disappeared.

一					
二 二					
三 三 三					
四 四 四 四 四					

五 (wǔ) • 六 (liù) • 七 (qī)

wǔ	Ancient Form	Later Form	Modern Form
five (4 strokes)			五
	五 is seen by some to resemble our numeral five (5). I see a '5'; do you? Other explanations link the top and bottom horizontals to Yin Yang theory.		

liù	Ancient Form	Later Form	Modern Form
six (4 strokes)			六
	六 orginally represented a 'hut.' Pronounced identically to 'six,' the character 'hut' was borrowed to represent 'six.' An entirely new character was then created to represent 'hut.'		

qī	Ancient Form	Later Form	Modern Form
seven (2 strokes)			七
	七 orginally meant 'to cut.' The character for 'cut' was borrowed to mean 'seven.' To differentiate 'seven' from the number ten (十), the end of the vertical line was curved, like this: 七. The meaning 'to cut' was represented by a new character, 切 (qiē), with 'seven' on the side and 'knife' on the right.		

bā	Ancient Form	Later Form	Modern Form
eight (*2 strokes; notice the length of the second stroke; strokes should not touch*)	)(	)(	八
	In the ancient form, as the graph seems to make clear, 八 originally represented 'to divide.' In yet another application of the loan process, the character for 'divide' was borrowed for 'eight,' and a new character was created for the meaning 'divide,' with 'eight' on the top and 'knife' on the bottom (分).		

jiǔ	Ancient Form	Later Form	Modern Form
nine (*2 strokes; enjoy the flourish at the end of the first stroke*)	乙	九	九
	Look closely at 九 and you can find the next number, 十 (*shí*). One story has it that 九 was 'bent' to suggest approaching the limit, 十 being the limit, and so one gets 'nine.' Others see 九 as a loan character from the word for 'elbow.'		

shí	Ancient Form	Later Form	Modern Form
ten (*2 strokes; horizontal first*)	│	十	十
	十 represents 'complete; fullness,' something extending in all 'ten' directions, the best there is, and thus, similar to our feeling about the number 'ten,' the highest score, a perfect ten.		

八	八			
九	九			
十	十			

火 (huǒ)

huǒ	Ancient Form	Later Form	Modern Form
fire (*4 strokes; an important radical*)	🔥	火	火

The character 火 (*huǒ*, 'fire') is a pictographic character that, in ancient times and now as well, depicts a flame. 火 is one of the most common radicals, appearing elongated when on the side of a multi-component character, such as in 煙/烟 (*yān*, 'smoke'), or as four separate strokes, such as in 熱/热 (*rè*, 'hot') when on the bottom of the character. 火 appears in many single characters relating to fire, heat, anger, or by extension, temper.

shāo	*yān*	*rè*	*jiān*
燒/烧	煙/烟	熱/热	煎
to burn	smoke	hot	to fry in shallow oil

火 in compound words:

火車 / 火车 fire + vehicle = 'train'	火藥 / 火药 fire + medicine = 'gunpowder'
火山 fire + mountain = 'volcano'	發火 / 发火 emit + fire = 'to get angry'

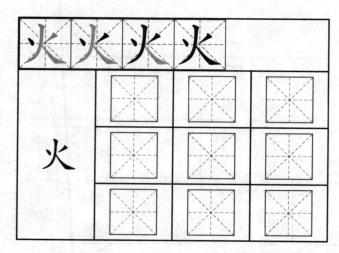

口 (kǒu)

kǒu	Ancient Form	Later Form	Modern Form
mouth (*3 strokes; an important radical*)			口

The character 口 (*kǒu*, 'mouth'), a pictographic character, is a drawing of an open mouth, or perhaps a 'smiling mouth,' in the ancient form. 口 is one of the most common radicals, usually appearing on the side of the character, or in words relating to the mouth, parts of the mouth, actions of the mouth, and speech. For example:

chī	shé	chǎo	yǎ	tǔ
吃	舌	吵	啞/哑	吐
to eat	tongue	to quarrel	dumb, mute	to spit

口 in compound words:

口音 mouth + sound = accent	口味 mouth + taste = flavor of food
口水 mouth + water = saliva	人口 person + mouths = population

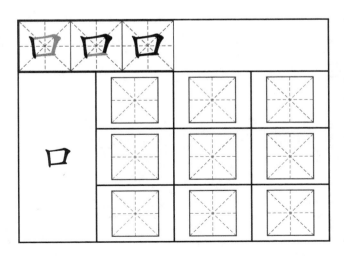

木 (mù)

mù	Ancient Form	Later Form	Modern Form
tree (4 strokes; an important radical)			木

The character 木 (mù, 'tree'), another pictographic character, is a drawing of a tree, complete with roots and branches. 木 is a common radical, appearing in characters or words relating to tree, wood, timber, wooden, or, by extension, numb or dull-witted, wooden-headed. For example:

sēn	chuáng	zhī	yǐ
森	床	枝	椅
forest	bed	branch; twig	chair

木 in compound words:

木工 wood + work = 'carpentry'	木馬 / 木马 wood + horse = (child's) 'rocking horse'
木屋 wood + room; house = 'log cabin'	麻木 numb + wood = 'numb'

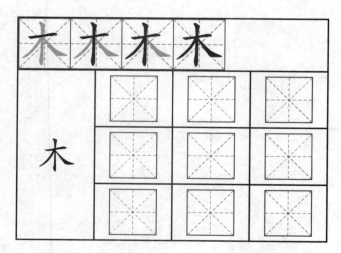

人 (*rén*)

rén	Ancient Form	Later Form	Modern Form
human being (*2 strokes; a very common important radical*)			人

The character 人 (*rén*, 'human being') depicts a side view of a person. 人 is an important radical appearing in characters relating to mankind, human action, and so on. As an independent character, it appears as 人, or, more commonly, as 亻 ('standing man'), a combining form in component characters. For example:

nǐ	*zuò*	*jiàn*	*zhòng*	*cóng*
你	做	健	眾/众	從/从
you	to do	health	crowd; the masses	to follow

人 in compound words:

人才 person + talent = 'a talented person'	人口 person + mouths = 'population'
家人 home + person = 'family member'	愛人 / 爱人 love + person = 'spouse' (male or female)

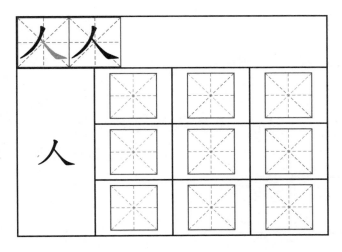

山 (shān)

shān	Ancient Form	Later Form	Modern Form
mountain (3 strokes; an important radical)			山

The character 山 (*shān*, 'mountain') is a drawing of several mountain peaks. 山 is a common radical appearing, as one would expect, in characters or words relating to mountain, slopes, hills, and so on. Notice where the radical appears.

gǎng	*àn*	*fēng*	*chóng*	*yì*
崗/岗	岸	峰	崇	屹
hillock	shore, bank	summit	high, sublime	towering

山 in compound words:

山水 mountain + water = 'landscape'	火山 fire + mountain = 'volcano'
山口 mountain + mouth = 'mountain pass'	大山 big + mountain = 'big mountain'

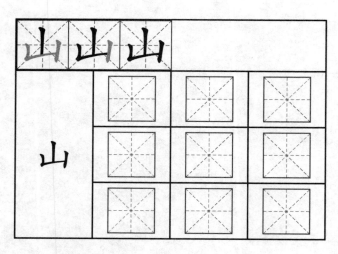

水 (shuǐ)

shuǐ	Ancient Form	Later Form	Modern Form
water (4 strokes; an important radical)			水

The character 水 (shuǐ, 'water') depicts flowing water. 水 is one of the most common radicals, appearing as 水 or 氵 (as a combining form usually on the left side) in characters related to water, bodies of water, or most anything dealing with liquids.

zhī	hàn	tāng	hé	lèi	hàn
汁	汗	湯/汤	河	淚/泪	漢/汉
juice	sweat	soup	river	tears	name of a Chinese dynasty; the Chinese people

水 in compound words:

水果 watery + fruit = 'fruit'	水平 water + level = 'horizontal'
水兵 water + soldier = 'sailor'	開水 / 开水 open + water = 'boiling/boiled water'

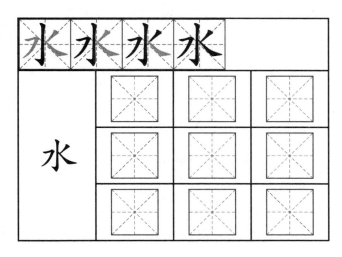

Unit 1

Get acquainted with the characters of this unit by reading over this list several times. You should be fluent before beginning writing practice. To test yourself, cover the English and see if you can understand the Chinese, and then cover the Chinese and translate the English into Chinese.

你好!		Hello!
好嗎?	好吗?	How are you?
好不好?		Are you well?
請你……	请你……	Would you please…?
是我。		It's me.
你好嗎?	你好吗?	How have you been?
不是我。		It's not me.
再見!	再见!	Goodbye!
對不起!	对不起!	Pardon me!
謝謝!	谢谢!	Thanks!
不謝.	不谢!	You're welcome!
姓謝.	姓谢.	My last name is Xie.
不姓謝.	不姓谢.	My last name is not Xie.
他們好嗎?	他们好吗?	Are they well?
你叫甚麼?	你叫什么?	What's your name?
他名字是……		His name is….
我叫 John.		My name is John.

Some Basic Terms

Simplified vs. Traditional or Complex Characters

Recall that simplified characters are those characters among the thousands of characters 'traditionally' used in Chinese that were selected by a government language committee shortly after the birth of the People's Republic to be simplified—that is, made easier to write by a reduction in their strokes. Most underwent modest changes, while a few others changed considerably. Here are two examples drawn from characters you have learned or will soon learn:

Traditional form	**After simplification**
見 (*jiàn*)	见 (*jiàn*)
幾 (*jǐ*)	几 (*jǐ*)

Pictographs (or Simplex) vs. Compound Characters

We use the term 'pictograph' to refer to characters that resemble what they mean, or at least used to. You've seen six already:

火，口，木，人，山，水, and also

一，二，三 and

上 (*shàng*)，下 (*xià*)

Different in structure from the characters above are what we term 'compound' characters—that is, characters that share common constituents or combining forms. These common combining forms were historically selected on the basis of meaning (now usually called *radicals* or meaning clues) and *phonetics* (sound clues) and combined together. A few hundred individual constituents joined in countless ways account for perhaps three-quarters of all characters.

Some examples: When you combine

'female' (radical) and 'horse' (phonetic): you get 媽/妈 (*mā*, 'mom');

'insect' (radical) and 'horse' (phonetic): you get 螞/蚂 (*mǎ*, 'ant');

'two mouths' and 'horse': you get 罵/骂 (*mà*, 'to curse'); and so on.

The vast majority of Chinese characters are compounds of meaning and sound.

Learn as many constituents as you can. These sheets will help you. Caution: the meaning and sound clues are usually generic in nature and not always reliable, especially the phonetic ones. The examples above present a reliable phonetic (*ma*) and a clearly identifiable radical. Not all characters will have such reliable clues. Nonetheless, there are clues, and they make what is a very difficult task less difficult. We urge your constant attention to such building blocks of characters during your study of Chinese, now and later.

Loan Words / Graphs

Some meanings are resistant to either 'picturing' (as in 'pictographs') or 'compounding' (combinations of two or more). For example, how does one picture the word 'no'? In many such cases, the language resorted to finding an already existing word (that is, existing character) pronounced just like the needed word, and borrowed that character to represent the written form of the hard-to-picture word. Example: 不 (*bú/bù*) means 'no.' Some scholars claim it originally represented a 'bird soaring into the sky.' Since 'a soaring bird' was pronounced in the spoken language nearly or exactly the same as 'no, not,' why not use 不 (*bú/bù*) to mean 'no, not'? Context usually helped determine which meaning was intended—thus the term 'loan character' or 'loan graph.' Such characters have little or no meaning or sound clues for learners. Learning them might take a bit more effort.

好 (hǎo)

hǎo	Ancient Form	Later Form	Modern Form
good, well, fine	𡥀	𭥀	好
Nǐ hǎo!			你好!

好 (*hǎo*, 'good') is formed with two components, a kneeling woman 女 (*nǚ*), the radical, on the left, with a child 子 (*zǐ*) on the right. In ancient China, indeed in all societies, a child born of a woman leads to all sorts of good things. Thus the meaning, and perhaps a useful memory aid and some cultural insight, given the importance of family continuance in China. By the way, if our 'etymologies' aren't helpful, we encourage you to make up your own to assist your recall. It's an important learning tactic and perhaps the more fanciful, the more 'yours,' the better.

• 你好! 我叫 Lynn.	• 你好! 我叫Lynn.
• *Chén Fēng*, 你好吗?	• *Chén Fēng*, 你好吗?
• 您 (*nín*) 好, *Zhōu Lǎoshī!*	• 您 (*nín*) 好, *Zhōu Lǎoshī!*
• 他也好吗?	• 他也好吗?

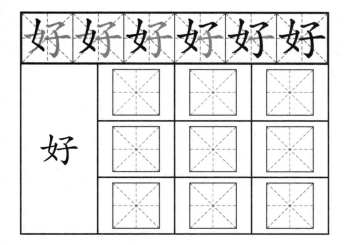

嗎/吗 (*ma*)

ma	Ancient Form	Modern Traditional Form	Modern Simplified Form
(*question particle*)	嗎	嗎	吗
Nǐ hǎo ma?		你好嗎?	你好吗?

嗎/吗 (*ma*) is a compound character in both its traditional and simplified forms. The left-side radical or semantic-meaning component is a 口 (*kǒu*, 'mouth'), indicating something spoken (a spoken question?), while on the right is the reliable phonetic/sound component 馬/马 (*mǎ*, 'horse'). Can you make out a 'horse,' with its front legs kicking up dust, and maybe a rider on top? Notice how the simplified form derives nicely from the traditional. 嗎/吗 is a final particle used in yes/no or rhetorical questions.

• 校长, 您忙 (*máng*, 'busy') 嗎? (校长, *xiàozhǎng*, 'principal')   • 你是美國人 (*Měiguó rén*, 'American') 嗎?   • 他姓 (*xìng*, 'be surnamed') Smith 嗎?   • 你不懂 (*dǒng*, 'understand') 嗎?
• 校长, 您忙 (*máng*, 'busy') 吗? (校长, *xiàozhǎng*, 'principal')   • 你是美国人 (*Měiguó rén*, 'American') 吗?   • 他姓 (*xìng*, 'be surnamed') Smith 吗?   • 你不懂 (*dǒng*, 'understand') 吗?

Modern Traditional Form	Modern Simplified Form
嗎 嗎 嗎 嗎 嗎 嗎 嗎 嗎 嗎 嗎 嗎 嗎 嗎	吗 吗 吗 吗 吗 吗
嗎	吗

請 / 请 (qǐng)

qǐng	Ancient Form	Modern Traditional Form	Modern Simplified Form
'will you please…,' request, ask; invite	請	請	请
Nín qǐng!		您請!	您请!

請/请 (*qǐng*, 'please') is another typical component character. Keep in mind that the majority of Chinese characters are of this type. On the left of this character is the radical/significant/semantic component 言 (*yán*, 'speech'), since when one requests, asks, or invites, it is often done through speech. Notice that its two-stroke simplified equivalent (讠) is simplified from seven strokes (言) to two and is derived from a common, handwritten form. On the right is the phonetic component 青 (*qīng*, 'blue' or 'green'), quite a reliable sound clue for this character, and for several other characters. 青 is very useful as a phonetic. Learn 青 and be more able (in the future, not now!) to recall the pronunciation of the following:

清	晴	情	鯖	蜻	氰
qīng	*qíng*	*qíng*	*qīng*	*qīng*	*qíng*
clear (as liquid)	clear (as weather)	sentiment	mackerel	dragonfly	cyanic acid

• 您請! ('Please go ahead of me!') • 老師, 請問 (*qǐngwèn*), 您叫甚麼名字 (*míngzi*, 'name')? ('Teacher, may I ask, what is your name?')	• 您请! ('Please go ahead of me!') • 老师, 请问 (*qǐngwèn*), 您叫什么名字 (*míngzi*, 'name')? ('Teacher, may I ask, what is your name?')

請/请 also appears in the following words:

我請你! / 我请你! 'My treat! / It's on me!'	請問 / 请问 please + ask = 'May I please ask…?'
您請! / 您请! (ask someone to go ahead of you; often repeated: 请, 请)	請客 / 请客 invite + guest = 'stand treat; give a party'

Modern Traditional Form	Modern Simplified Form

請 請 請 請 請 請
請 請 請 請 請 請
請 請 請

請

请 请 请 请 请
请 请 请 请

请

你 (nǐ)

nǐ	Ancient Form	Modern Form
you (*singular*)	伱	你
Nǐ hǎo!		你好!

你 (*nǐ*, 'you') is a typical compound character (two side-by-side components) where one side, the radical (on the left side in most characters), indicates broad meaning, while the other side is a clue (not always reliable but often a clue nonetheless) to pronunciation. On the left of 你 is the radical, 亻 ('person,' standing or in profile [full form: 人]). On the right is the phonetic component 尔 (*mǐ*). It is not at all a fully reliable sound hint, but maybe it offers something for our attention. *mǐ > mǐ > mǐ > nǐ*! By the way, when 尔 functions as an independent character (not a phonetic component) it is pronounced *ěr*.

• 你好!	• 你好!
• 你們好.	• 你们好.
• 你叫甚麼?	• 你叫什么?
• 你們都 (*dōu*) 是美國人嗎?	• 你们都 (*dōu*) 是美国人吗?

你 你 你 你 你 你
你

你

是 (shì)

shì	Ancient Form	Later Form	Modern Form
be; be so; yes	𱗋	𱗋	是
Shì bú shì?			是不是?

是 (*shì*, 'to be') is an equative verb formed with a 日 (*rì*, 'sun' [slightly flattened]) on top and 正 (*zhèng*, 'correct' [altered]) on bottom. When the sun brings something to light, it results in truth, something correct, something that's so. Maybe that can serve as a memory aid.

你是中國人嗎？ 　—是。我是中國人。 Lynn, 這位是楊老師. ('Lynn, this is Prof. Yang.')	你是中国人吗？ 　—是。我是中国人。 Lynn, 这位是杨老师. ('Lynn, this is Prof. Yang.')

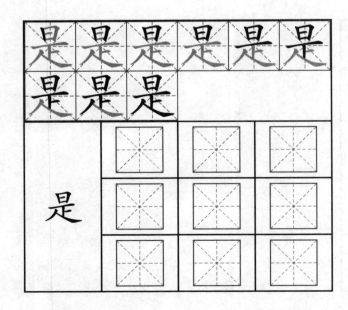

　Copyright © 2012 by Yale University and China International Publishing Group

我 (wǒ)

wǒ	Ancient Form	Later Form	Modern Form
I; me	𢎨	我	我
Wǒ hěn hǎo.			我很好.

我 (*wǒ*, 'I; me'), which appears as if it didn't have two parts, actually does. It is a picture of a hand, 手 (*shǒu*) (on the left), 'personally' holding one's own ancient weapon, a halberd or lance (戈). You'll realize the two parts when you practice writing 我. The form was later used exclusively to mean 'I; me.'

• 我姓陳(*Chén*).	• 我姓陈(*Chén*).
• 請問, 您貴姓? (*Qǐng wèn, nín guìxìng?*)	• 请问, 您贵姓? (*Qǐng wèn, nín guìxìng?*)
• 我叫*Máo Zhìpéng*, 我是北京人. (*Běijīng rén*)	• 我叫*Máo Zhìpéng*, 我是北京人. (*Běijīng rén*)

(Don't forget the dot, the final stroke of the 'lance.')

再 (zài)

zài	Ancient Form	Later Form	Modern Form
again	𩵋	再	再
zàijiàn			再見／再见

再 (zài) means 'again, for a second time.' The ancient form is a fish in the middle with two horizontal lines on the ends indicating two fish on a line. Two fish on a line > 'again; twice; once more.' What then of the modern form? Any clues there? Some see a 'structure' with layer upon layer, 'again' and 'again' (those three horizontal lines, perhaps?). You can take your choice or provide another to remember 再's meaning of 'again.'

• 王 (*Wáng*, surname) 老師，再見！ • 王老師，請您再說一遍 (*yí biàn*)。	• 王 (*Wáng*, surname) 老师，再见！ • 王老师，请您再说一遍 (*yí biàn*)。

再 also appears in the following words:

再見／再见 again + see = 'good-bye; see you again'	再三 again + three = 'over and over again'

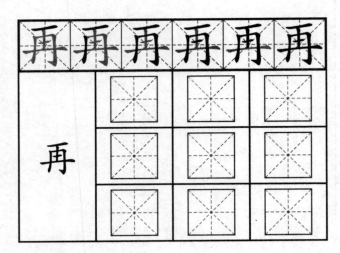

jiàn	Ancient Form	Later Form	Modern Traditional Form	Modern Simplified Form
see; meet up with	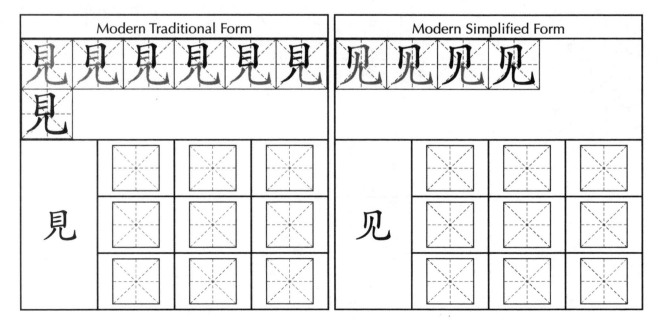		見	见
Zàijiàn!			再見!	再见!

見/见 (*jiàn*) combines a large 目 (*mù*, 'eye') on top of an altered 人 (*rén*, 'person') and easily renders the meaning 'to see,' or the extended meaning 'to go to see; to meet up with.' Like many simplified characters, the modern simplified form derives from the common hand-written form. Many commonly used handwritten forms, popular for many years among the people, became official simplified characters, so the transition to simplified characters was a relatively easy task for native speakers of Chinese. Our task as second language learners is not so easy.

• 再見 Lynn!
• 明天 (*míngtiān*, 'tomorrow') 見.
• 一會兒 (*yí huìr*, 'little while') 見.
• 李老師 (*Lǐ Lǎoshī*, 'teacher') 再見!

• 再见 Lynn!
• 明天 (*míngtiān*, 'tomorrow') 见.
• 一会儿 (*yí huìr*, 'little while') 见.
• 李老师 (*Lǐ Lǎoshī*, 'teacher') 再见!

Modern Traditional Form	Modern Simplified Form
見 見 見 見 見 見 見	见 见 见 见

對/对 (duì)

duì	Ancient Form	Later Form	Modern Traditional Form	Modern Simplified Form
face toward; correct	対	對	對	对
Duìbuqǐ!			對不起!	对不起!

The ancient form of 對/对 (*duì*) is a hand on the right holding a stand upon which candles burn. Look closely at the earlier forms, and the modern traditional forms for the candles and the hand (the candles disappeared in the simplified form). Perhaps this is the origin for the meaning 'face toward' (the burning candles, that is). 對不起/对不起 (*duìbuqǐ*) literally means 'one cannot (不) rise (起) to face (對/对) the other person,' so one is unworthy and needs to excuse oneself. From the original meaning of 'toward,' the meaning of 'correct,' and, in certain contexts 'yes,' was also derived, all from the character 對/对.

對不起, 我不懂. 　—没關系, 我再说一遍. (*Méi guānxì, wǒ zài shuō yí biàn.*) 對不對? 對. 'Right or wrong? Right.'	对不起, 我不懂. 　—没关系, 我再说一遍. (*Méi guānxì, wǒ zài shuō yí biàn.*) 对不对? 对. 'Right or wrong? Right.'

Modern Traditional Form	Modern Simplified Form
對 對 對 對 對 對 對 對 對 對 對 對 對 對 對	对 对 对 对 对 对

　Copyright © 2012 by Yale University and China International Publishing Group

不 (bù)

bù	Ancient Form	Later Form	Modern Form
not; no	𣎵	𣎵	不

In ancient times 不 (*bù*, 'not, no') was a drawing of a bird rising to heaven, no longer in sight. Other sources claim it originally represented a 'radish.' The Chinese language, needing a word to represent the negative, borrowed the character meaning 'radish' and used it to mean 'no, not,' in the process known as 'phonetic loan.' My real dislike for radishes led me to forming a memory aid for '*bù*.' NO radishes for me! Reminder: 不 (just like 一, *yī*, 'one') changes its tone in certain environments. Do you remember the rule?

• 不好 — 不對 — 是不是? • 不謝 — 對不起! • 我不姓王. • 他不是老師, 他是學生. (學生, *xuéshēng*, 'student')	• 不好 — 不对 — 是不是? • 不谢 — 对不起! • 我不姓王. • 他不是老师, 他是学生. (学生, *xuéshēng*, 'student')

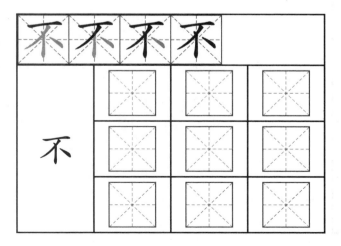

起 (*qǐ*)

qǐ	Ancient Form	Modern Form
get up; rise; start	起	起
Duìbuqǐ!		對不起/对不起!

起 (*qǐ*) is composed of two components, a signific indicating broad meaning and a phonetic, roughly indicating sound. On the left is the common character 走 (*zǒu*), meaning 'walk, go,' a common radical. On the right of 起 is the phonetic component 己 (*jǐ*). *jǐ > jǐ > jǐ > qǐ*!

(After bumping into someone) 對不起, 對不起! 　—沒關系, 沒關系! (*Méi guānxì*) 'No problem!/That's quite all right!'	(After bumping into someone) 对不起, 对不起! 　—没关系, 没关系! (*Méi guānxì*) 'No problem!/That's quite all right!'

起 also appears in the following words:

對不起/对不起 face (a person) + (can)not + rise to = 'sorry'	一起 one + rise = 'together' 起床 rise + bed = 'to get out of bed; to get up in the morning'

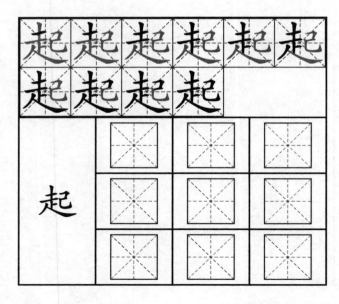

　　Copyright © 2012 by Yale University and China International Publishing Group

姓 (*xìng*)

xìng	Ancient Form	Later Form	Modern Form
surname(d); family name	𡥑	𡣘	姓
Tā xìng shénme?			他姓甚麼／什么?

姓 (*xìng*, 'surname[d]') is formed with 女 (*nǚ*, 'woman') on the left, the radical (somewhat elongated when a radical), and 生 (*shēng*; 'give birth'), on the right, suggesting a child is born (生) of a woman (女) and thus acquires a surname. In ancient times, it was the mother from whom one derived one's family name. In present-day China, a woman retains her family name after marriage rather than adopting the man's name, as is common in many other cultures.

他姓甚麼? ——他姓謝. 請問, 您貴姓?	他姓什么? ——他姓谢. 请问, 您贵姓?

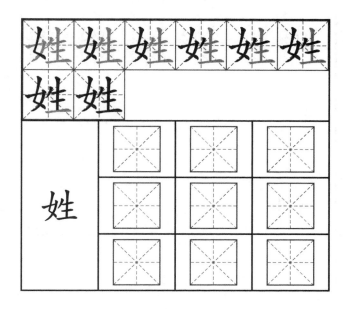

謝/谢 (*xiè*)

xiè	Ancient Form	Modern Traditional Form	Modern Simplified Form
thank; (*a surname*)	謝	謝	谢
xièxie!		謝謝!	谢谢!

謝/谢 (*xiè*, 'to thank') 謝謝/谢谢 (*xièxie*, 'thank you'). On the left is the speech radical, (言/讠), and on the right is the phonetic component 射 (*shè*, 'shoot'), a long way from *xiè* to be sure. 謝/谢 may provide an early example of a character for which it is difficult to find a memory aid. 'Speech' plus 'shoot'? Perhaps you can suggest one. If you can, let me say 謝謝/谢谢 to you! Here's a fun expression using 謝/谢: 謝天謝地/谢天谢地 (*xiè tiān xiè dì*) ('thank heaven and thank earth') = Thank goodness! / Thank God!

• 謝謝您!
• 謝謝你!
• 謝謝老師!
• 不謝, 不謝.

• 谢谢您!
• 谢谢你!
• 谢谢老师!
• 不谢, 不谢.

Modern Traditional Form	Modern Simplified Form
謝 謝 謝 謝 謝 謝	谢 谢 谢 谢 谢 谢
謝 謝 謝 謝 謝 謝	谢 谢 谢 谢 谢 谢
謝 謝 謝 謝 謝	
謝	谢

他 (tā)

tā	Ancient Form	Modern Form
he; him	爬	他
Tā hěn hǎo.		他很好.

他 (*tā*, 'he; him') combines the very common radical for 人 (*rén*, 'man; person') (the 'standing-man' variety, 亻) with a very old phonetic, pronounced nowadays nothing like '*tā*.' The right side is actually a common character you have either learned already or will soon learn. It's 也 (*yě*, 'also'). You will need to distinguish:

      也 (*yě*)   also
      他 (*tā*)   he; him
      她 (*tā*)   she; her (with 女, *nǚ*, 'female' radical)

他好嗎? 　—他很好, 你呢? 我也好.	他好吗? 　—他很好, 你呢? 我也好.

他 also appears in the following words:

他的 he + 的 (*de*) = 'his'	他很好. He is well.
他们 he + (plural suffix) = 'they' (including men and women)	

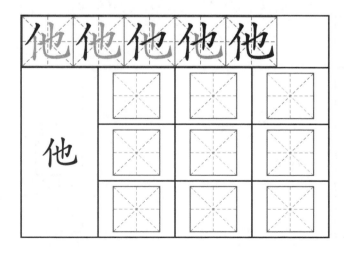

們/们 (*men*)

men	Ancient Form	Modern Traditional Form	Modern Simplified Form
(plural suffix for nouns and pronouns)	們	們	们
wǒmen, nǐmen, tāmen		我們, 你們, 他們	我们, 你们, 他们

們/们 (*men*) (note: no tone) is a compound character built, like the majority of Chinese characters, of two components: on the left is the radical, 亻 (*rén*), meaning 'man,' a 'person' (this 'combining form' is often referred to as 'a standing man' [full shape: 人]); on the right is the very reliable sound indicator or phonetic 門/门 (*mén*, 'door'). Looks like a door with two (multiple or plural) leaves, right? 們/们 is added to a pronoun or noun, usually related to persons, indicating plurality.

• 我們都好, 你們呢? • 他們都懂, 你也懂嗎?	• 我们都好, 你们呢? • 他们都懂, 你也懂吗?

們/们 also appears in the following words:

我 (I) + 們/们 = 我們/我们 'we'	你 (you) + 們/们 = 你們/你们 'you' [*plural*]
他 (he) + 們/们 = 他們/他们 　　'they/them'	孩子 (child) + 們/们 = 孩子們/孩子们 　　'children'

Modern Traditional Form	Modern Simplified Form
們 們 們 們 們 們 們 們 們 們	们 们 们 们 们
們	们

叫 (jiào)

jiào	Ancient Form	Modern Form
be called (by a name)	叫 (ancient)	叫
Nǐ jiào shénme?		你叫甚麼/什么?

叫 (*jiào*, 'to be called') combines the very common radical 口 (*kǒu*, 'mouth') on the left—which implies some sort of activity involved with speech—with 丩 (*jiū*) on the right, which provides a clue to its sound. The right side looks like the number 'four,' right? Memory aid: "I called you four times and you still haven't answered!" 口 is an important radical, well worth remembering. You will see it again and again (e.g., in 叫, 嗎/吗, 名).

請問, 你叫甚麼名字? —我姓李 (*Lǐ*), 叫李文 (*Lǐ Wén*). 我叫 John, 你叫甚麼?	请问, 你叫什么名字? —我姓李 (*Lǐ*), 叫李文 (*Lǐ Wén*). 我叫 John, 你叫什么?

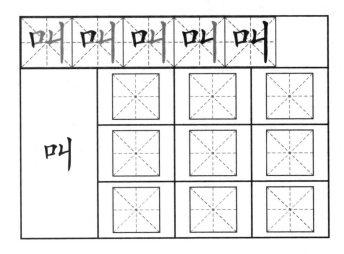

甚/什 (shén)

shén	Ancient Form	Modern Traditional Form	Modern Simplified Form
(combining form with 'me' [麼/么]); what?	什	甚	什
shénme?		甚麼?	什么?

甚/什 (shén), in its simplified form, combines 'person' (rén, the 'standing man' [full form 人]) on the left with 十 (shí, 'ten') on the right, with the original meaning of 'ten people.' Note how the modern simplified form actually resembles the ancient form. Later 甚/什 came to be used with 麼/么 (me) to mean 'what,' 甚么/什么 (shénme). Note that, when pronounced, the 'n' of shénme disappears and it is pronounced as if spelled 'shémme.' This is a pinyin convention that you have to get used to.

• 他叫甚麼名字?	• 他叫什么名字?
• 他名字叫謝立山 (Lìshān).	• 他名字叫谢立山 (Lìshān).
• 他姓甚麼, 叫甚麼?	• 他姓什么, 叫什么?
• 你的電話號碼 (diànhuà hàomǎ) 是甚麼?	• 你的电话号码 (diànhuà hàomǎ) 是什么?
What's your telephone number?	What's your telephone number?

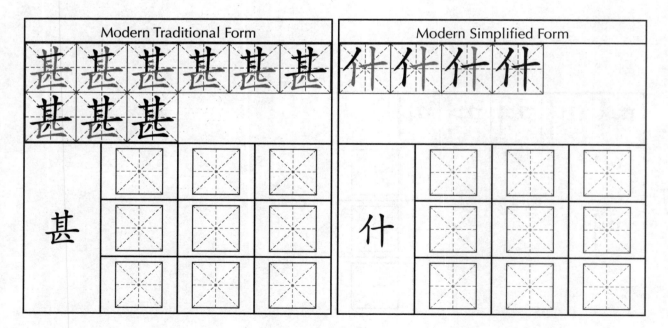

麼／么 (*me*)

me	Ancient Form	Modern Traditional Form	Modern Simplified Form
(suffix to the question word and adverb 'what, how')	麼	麼	么
shénme		甚麼	什么

麼／么 (*me*) as a suffix is a phonetic loan; that is, a character with near identical pronunciation but a different meaning was 'borrowed' to serve as a needed character. Note how the simplified form is simply a reduction to the bottom part of the traditional character. On the bottom of both characters, traditional and simplified, there's something that looks like a 'nose'—someone sniffing to find out 'what' something is, what's going on.

• 你叫甚麼名字？	• 你叫什么名字？
• 你説 (*shuō*, 'say') 甚麼？	• 你说 (*shuō*, 'say') 什么？

麼／么 also appears in the following words:

甚麼／什么 — 'what?'	多麼／多么 — 'how, what' (to express exclamation)
怎麼／怎么— 'how?'	這麼／这么 — 'such, so'

Modern Traditional Form	Modern Simplified Form
麼 麼 麼 麼 麼 麼 麼 麼 麼 麼 麼 麼 麼 麼	么 么 么
麼	么

名 (*míng*)

míng	Ancient Form	Later Form	Modern Form
name	叩	召	名
míngzi			名字

名 (*míng*, 'name') is composed of 口 (*kǒu*, 'mouth' radical) on the bottom and 'evening' on top. Perhaps the reasoning is: In the dark of the evening a person can only be identified by shouting his/her name. By the way, the element for 'evening' (the top part) is worth noticing. It appears in another very useful character: 多 (*duō*) [evening on top of evening] > 'many; numerous.' You will learn it in the next unit.

• 他叫甚麼名字.	• 他叫什么名字.
• 他姓 *Mèng*, 叫 *Mèng Dérú*.	• 他姓 *Mèng*, 叫 *Mèng Dérú*.

名 also appears in the following words:

名人 (name + person) = 'a famous person; celebrity'	名字 (name + character) = 'name; given name'
有名 (have + name) = 'famous'	姓名 (surname + given name) = 'one's full name'

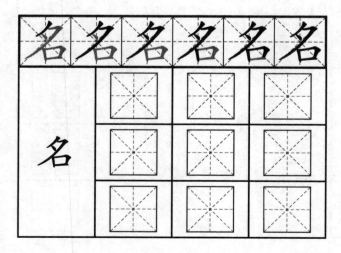

字 (zì)

zì	Ancient Form	Later Form	Modern Form
written character; word	㝸	宋	字
míngzi			名字

字 (*zì*, 'written character; word') is composed of ⼧ ('roof') on top and 子 (*zǐ*, 'child') underneath. 子 also supplies a reliable clue to pronunciation (but not for the tone; accurate tonal 'carryover' is rarely the case with the phonetic component). The original meaning of 字 was 'to give birth at home.' You may see that clearly in the ancient form. Well, after the birth of a child, what's one of the first thing parents do? Give the child a name, of course. In this unit we see 字 as part of the word 名字 (*míngzi*, 'name; given name'). Still later, 字 was borrowed to mean a 'written character' or 'word,' which is now its most common meaning as a single character, but not, however, part of this unit's vocabulary, although a very useful item. Memory aid for 字: 'a child practicing writing characters at home.'

字 also appears in the following words:

生字 give birth to + character = 'new character, new word' (to be learned)	請問, 你叫甚麼名字 / 请问, 你叫什么名字? 'May I ask your name?'

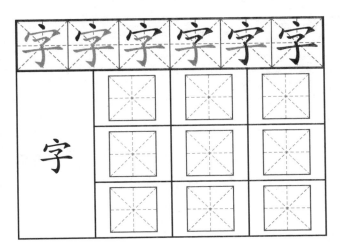

Unit 2

Get acquainted with the characters of this unit by reading over this list several times. You should be fluent before beginning writing practice. To test yourself, cover the English and see if you can understand the Chinese, and then cover the Chinese and translate the English into Chinese.

你几岁？	你幾歲？	How old are you? (*said to a child*)
哪年？		Which year?
地址		address
你多大了？		How old are you?
几月几号？	幾月幾號？	What's the date?
那位老师	那位老師	that teacher
出生		be born
您好！		Hello! How do you do?
这儿; 那儿; 哪儿？	這兒; 那兒; 哪兒？	here; there; where?
我的名字		my name
号码	號碼	number
他很小.		He's very young.
这是什么？	這是甚麼？	What is this?

More on Chinese Character Building

In the last unit we talked about characters that, at one time at least, resembled the reality that they represented, much as a painting resembles a scene. Soon the need arose to find written symbols for meanings that could not be illustrated by a simple picture. Sure, it was relatively easy to draw a picture of the sun or the moon or an eye, but what about representing 'to open one's eyes'? A solution was found by compounding, joining two existing characters to create a new one. To represent 'to open the eyes' in writing, an existing character whose pronunciation was identical was borrowed for the new character. To this phonetic or 'pronunciation' part was added a 'meaning marker' (now called a 'radical'), in order to distinguish the new character from the old one. Here's how we think the character for 'to open one's eyes' came into being:

semantic	+	phonetic	=	new character
目		争/争		睁/睁
mù		*zhēng*		*zhēng*
'eye'		(phonetic)		'to open one's eyes'

By means of this method, the 'semantic-phonetic principle,' thousands of characters were created. Most of the characters that exist today are of this type. Another method of character construction, again with compounding, involved combining two constituents whose meanings supported one another.

constituent one	+	constituent two	=	new character
女		子		好
nǚ		*zǐ*		*hǎo*
'woman'		'son'		'good'

Finally, another wave of borrowing took place involving simply borrowing an existing character to stand in for one that did not exist. So, the existing character 那 (*nà/nèi*), which was used for the name of an ancient state, was borrowed to write the word 'that,' which had the same pronunciation.

The end result was a language with thousands of characters. An average Chinese dictionary contains about 6,000 single characters, plus many tens of thousands more of words made up of combining two or more characters into multi-syllabic words.

您 (*nín*)

nín	Ancient Form	Modern Form
you (*respectful*)	悠	您
Nín hǎo!		您好!

您 (*nín*, 'you') is, thankfully, one character that provides some clues regarding its components. You see on the top of 您 the character 你 (*nǐ*), which you met in Unit 1 (你好!). The bottom component is 心 (*xīn*, 'heart'). So 您 is 你 with a good deal of 'heart' 心. Use 您 when you address someone of rank with 'heartfelt' respect.

• 老師, 您好!	• 老师, 您好!
• 老師, 您是哪年生的?	• 老师, 您是哪年生的?
• 老師, 您是屬 (*shǔ*, 'belong to' [one of the 12 cyclical signs]) 甚麼的?	• 老师, 您是属 (*shǔ*, 'belong to' [one of the 12 cyclical signs]) 什么的?

您 您 您 您 您 您
您 您 您 您 您

您

大 (dà)

dà	Ancient Form	Modern Form
big; older in age	大	大
Nǐ duō dà le?		你多大了?

大 (*dà*, 'big; older in age') is a representation of a person extending arms to express big, large, immense—something we've all done at one time or another. Some say that the drawing reflects ancient Chinese philosophy, with its view that the human being is the most powerful, most central, most important, and, therefore, the 'biggest' creature in the world.

你多大了? 　—我二十. 您呢? 您多大歲數 (*suìshu*, 　　'age') 了? 我七十五了.	你多大了? 　—我二十. 您呢? 您多大岁数 (*suìshu*, 　　'age') 了? 我七十五了.

大 also appears in the following words:

大人 large + person = 'adult'	大家 large + family = 'everybody, everyone'

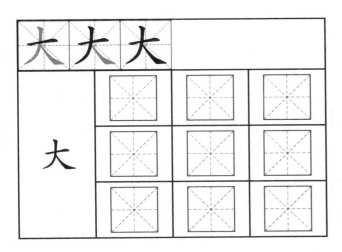

小 (xiǎo)

xiǎo	Ancient Form	Later Form	Modern Form
small; young			小
Tā hěn xiǎo.			他很小.

The early form of 小 (*xiǎo*, 'small; young') shows three grains of sand. It also suggests the meaning of 'divide' (one vertical 'dividing' two others), and when one divides, things are made smaller. Notice again how the first stroke (the middle one, mind you) intersects, divides, and therefore makes smaller, leading to the modern meaning 'small.' Remember, when writing, make the middle stroke first.

你弟弟幾歲了? (弟弟, *dìdì*, 'younger brother') 　—他三歲, 很小.	你弟弟几岁了? (弟弟, *dìdì*, 'younger brother') 　—他三岁, 很小.

小 also appears in the following words:

大小 large + small = 'size' (of something)	小人 small + person = 'low-class person'
小吃 small + eat = 'snack'	小心 small + heart = 'careful'

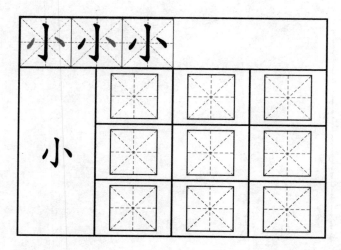

多 (duō)

duō	Ancient Form	Modern Form
many; much	 	多
Nǐ duō dà le?		你多大了?

夕 in 多 (*duō*) means 'moon.' Two moons, one atop the other, is just too many for me. There's your clue. It also means 'evening.' So evening after evening led to the meaning 'many.'

你多大了? 　—我二十八了. 他呢? 　—他三歲. 很小.	你多大了? 　—我二十八了. 他呢? 　—他三岁. 很小.

多 (*duō*) in compound words and phrases:

多心 many + heart = 'oversensitive'	多謝 / 多谢 many + thank = 'thanks very much' (often repeated)
很多 very + many = 'a lot; numerous'	不多 not + many = 'few'

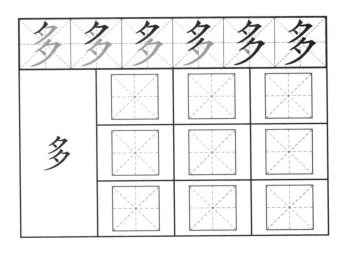

位 (wèi)

wèi	Ancient Form	Later Form	Modern Form
('polite' measure word for persons of rank, status)	企	位	位
sān wèi lǎoshī			三位老師/师

The ancient form of 位 (wèi) is a drawing of a person standing on the ground, pretty clear in the ancient form, at least. Later, it was used to represent the meaning of 'to stand' (the right side of the present character, 立, lì). Add the radical for 'person' on the left and we get the meaning of 'a person of standing,' now used as a measure word for persons of rank, such as your teacher, 老师 (lǎoshī), for whom you might 'stand' when addressing.

• 這位老師	• 这位老师
• 那位老師	• 那位老师
• 哪位老師?	• 哪位老师?
• 三位老師.	• 三位老师.
• 王老師, 您早!	• 王老师, 您早!

位 位 位 位 位 位
位

位

這/这 (*zhè/zhèi*)

zhè/zhèi	Ancient Form	Modern Traditional Form	Modern Simplified Form
this	這	這	这
Zhè shì shénme?		這是甚麼?	这是什么?

The character 這/这 (*zhè/zhèi*, 'this') is a phonetic loan. In this particular phonetic loan, the language needed to express 'this'—a challenging thing to picture. In such cases like 'this,' the language borrowed an existing character with an identical or near-identical sound. It's challenging to devise memory aids for such characters. In many cases, you simply need to memorize them. Earlier forms of this character appear to be also of little help. 這/这's direct opposite is 那 (*nà/nèi*). Both are commonly used specifiers ('this, that, these, those,' and so on). Have you got an idea for a memory aid for this character?

(pointing to a photo) 這位是你的甚麼人? 　　—是我的學生. 這是你的e-mail地址嗎? 　　—對了. 這是我的.	*(pointing to a photo)* 这位是你的什么人? 　　—是我的学生. 这是你的e-mail地址吗? 　　—对了. 这是我的.

Modern Traditional Form	Modern Simplified Form
這 這 這 這 這 這 這 這 這 這 這 這	这 这 这 这 这 这 这 这

那 (*nà / nèi*)

nà / nèi	Ancient Form	Modern Form
that		那
nà nián / nèi nián		那年

Originally the name of an ancient state in China, the character 那 (*nà/nèi*) now has the meaning of 'that,' which pairs with 'this' (這/这, *zhè/zhèi*), the two specifiers introduced in this unit.

• 那個 (*gè*) 是我的. ('That thing is mine.')	• 那个 (*gè*) 是我的. ('That thing is mine.')
• 那不對.	• 那不对.
• 那個是甚麼?	• 那个是什么?
• 那個電話號碼不是我的.	• 那个电话号码不是我的.

那 also appears in the following words:

那兒/那儿 that + *-er* suffix = 'there'	那些 that + some = 'those'
那麼/那么 that + *me* = 'so, then'	那個/那个 that + *ge* = 'that/that one'

那 那 那 那 那 那
那

哪 (nǎ / něi)

nǎ / něi	Modern Form
which; where	哪
Nǐ shì nǎ/něi nián shēng de?	你是哪年生的?

Here's a character for which you already know one component. Find 那 (*nà/nèi*, 'that') in this character. Now add the mouth radical 口 (*kǒu*), and the character shifts meaning from 'that' to 'which, where.' 口 is an important radical, well worth looking out for. It is used in many characters that have to do with something spoken.

Answer the following questions:

• 你是哪國人?	• 你是哪国人?
• 你家在哪兒/哪裡?	• 你家在哪儿/哪里?
• 你是哪年生的?	• 你是哪年生的?

哪 also appears in the following compound words:

哪個/哪个? interrogative + *ge* = 'which one'	哪位? interrogative + *wei* = 'which one, who'
哪兒/哪儿? interrogative + *-er* suffix = 'where'	哪裡/哪里 interrogative + inside, = 'where'
哪些 interrogative + several = 'which' (of several items)	

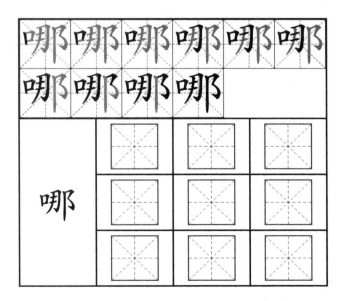

兒/儿 (ér)

ér	Ancient Form	Later Form	Modern Traditional Form	Modern Simplified Form
(-r suffix ending)			兒	儿
zhèr; nàr; nǎr			這兒; 那兒; 哪兒	这儿; 那儿; 哪儿

兒/儿 (ér [suffix]), as far as its relevance to this unit of *Encounters*, stands as a suffix providing the written representation of the 'r' sound in such words as 那兒/那儿 (nàr) 'there,' 這兒/这儿 (zhèr) 'here,' or 哪兒/哪儿 (nǎr) 'where,' as well as many others not yet introduced. This feature of pronunciation (adding the '-ér' suffix) is more common among speakers of Mandarin in north China, especially Beijing, and is introduced in most textbooks. It is interesting to note that when 兒/儿 appears in a compound word (rather than as a 'sound suffix'), it is pronounced ér and means 'son; baby; children; young man.'

兒女 / 儿女 (*érnǚ*) son + daughter = 'children'	女兒 / 女儿 (*nǚ'ér*) female + baby = 'daughter'
兒子 / 儿子 (*érzi*) son + baby = 'son'	

Modern Traditional Form	Modern Simplified Form
兒 兒 兒 兒 兒 兒 兒 兒	儿 儿

Copyright © 2012 by Yale University and China International Publishing Group

幾/几 (*jǐ*)

jǐ	Ancient Form	Modern Traditional Form	Modern Simplified Form
how many? *(usually for less than ten)*	絲	幾	几
Nǐ jǐ suì?		你幾歲?	你几岁?

The traditional form of 幾/几 (*jǐ*) originally meant 'on guard against small dangers.' Some see in the character 'soldiers on guard against all dangers, big or little.' The simplified form, greatly revised from the traditional, is actually a pictograph of a small table or stool. Eventually, the modern meaning evolved into 'how many' (but usually for 'smaller,' fewer, less than ten).

Answer the following questions:

• 你幾歲了?	• 你几岁了?
• 你的生日是幾月幾號?	• 你的生日是几月几号?
• 今天 (*jīntiān*, 'today') 幾月幾號?	• 今天 (*jīntiān*, 'today') 几月几号?

Modern Traditional Form	Modern Simplified Form
幾 幾 幾 幾 幾 幾	几 几
幾 幾 幾 幾 幾 幾	
幾	几

號/号 (*hào*)

hào	Ancient Form	Modern Traditional Form	Modern Simplified Form
number; order; rank; mark; sign	號 (ancient seal form)	號	号
hàomǎ		號碼	号码

The character 號/号 (*hào*) originally meant 'a tiger's howl.' The right component of the traditional character is a tiger and the left depicts a mouth emitting sound. The modern simplified form has 'lost the tiger' but retained the mouth, on top, sounding off. From 'to howl; to yell,' 號/号 extended its meaning to 'someone who shouts his name or title and therefore expresses his order or rank.'

今天幾號？ 　——一月一號 你家電話號碼是多少？ 　——四八二 九七三五	今天几号？ 　——一月一号 你家电话号码是多少？ 　——四八二 九七三五。

號/号 in compound words:

號碼 / 号码 number + code = 'number'	書號 / 书号 book + number = 'book number'
口號 / 口号 mouth + number = 'slogan'	問號 / 问号 question + mark = 'question mark'

Modern Traditional Form	Modern Simplified Form
號 號 號 號 號 號 號 號 號 號 號 號 號	号 号 号 号 号

了 *(le)*

le	Ancient Form	Modern Form
(particle used to express change of state or situation)	?	了
Wǒ hǎo le.		我好了.

The ancient form of 了 (*le*) is a drawing of a baby or child. In the meaning encountered in Unit 1, 了 is used to indicate a change of state or the realization of a change. Think of 昨天不好, 今天好了 (*Zuótiān bù hǎo, jīntiān hǎo le*). 'Yesterday I (or the weather or some situation) wasn't well; but today I'm/it's better.' For your memory aid, consider that as a child grows older, change is constant. By the way, distinguish 了 from 子 (*zǐ*, 'child'), the right-side component of 好 (*hǎo*, 'good').

你多大歲數了? (了 added perhaps because our age is constantly changing) —我七十五了. 你呢? 我也七十五了. 真巧! (*Zhēn qiǎo*, 'What a coincidence!')	你多大岁数了? (了 added perhaps because our age is constantly changing) —我七十五了. 你呢? 我也七十五了. 真巧! (*Zhēn qiǎo*, 'What a coincidence!')

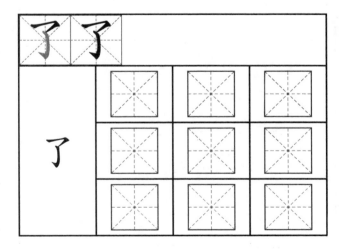

年 (nián)

nián	Ancient Forms	Modern Form
year	秂 秂	年
nǎ/něi nián?		哪年

Although the two parts are not easily distinguished, some claim that the top part (禾) of the ancient form of 年 (*nián*, 'year') meant 'grain,' while yet another part meant 'thousands' (the character 千 '*qiān*'). Others see the bottom as a form of the character 人 (*rén*), meaning 'person.' Perhaps you can you picture a person yearly carrying grain to market? That might help memory. Got a better idea?

你是哪年生的? 　—我是一九八七年生的.	你是哪年生的? 　—我是一九八七年生的.

年 also appears in the following words:

年月日 year + month + day = 'date' (on the calendar)	明年 bright + year = 'next year'
年年 year + year = 'every year, year after year'	年歲 / 年岁 year + year of age = 'age'

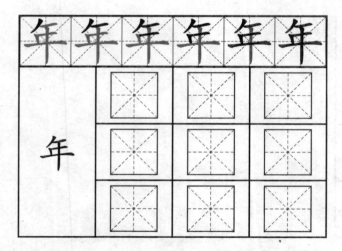

月 (yuè)

yuè	Ancient Form	Later Form	Modern Form
the moon; month			月
Jǐ yuè jǐ hào?			幾月幾號/ 几月几号

The character 月 (*yuè*, 'moon, month') is a drawing of the crescent moon. 月 is one of the most common radicals, and it appears in compound words relating to moon, month, bright, light, and time. For example, place 日 (*rì*, 'sun') beside 月 and one gets lots and lots of light and the meaning 'bright' (明, *míng*), used in 明天 (*míngtiān*, 'tomorrow').

你的生日是幾月幾號? 　　—我的生日是十二月十七號. 是嗎? 我的也是.	你的生日是几月几号? 　　—我的生日是十二月十七号. 是吗? 我的也是.

Can you recite the names of the months in Chinese? Do you know how your birthday is expressed in Chinese? In what year and month were you born?

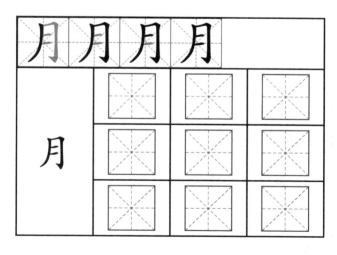

日 (rì)

rì	Ancient Form	Later Form	Modern Form
sun; day	⊙	⊖	日
shēngrì			生日

The character 日 ('sun') is a pictographic character drawing of the sun. 日 is one of the most common radicals appearing in characters or words relating to sun, sunshine, hot, light, day, and time.

dawn	past; old	morning; early	spring	evening; late	dry in the sun
旦	旧	早	春	晚	晒

日 in compound words:

日光 sun + light = 'sunlight'	日历 sun + experience = 'calendar'
日用 day + use = 'of everyday use'	生日 give birth + sun = 'birthday'

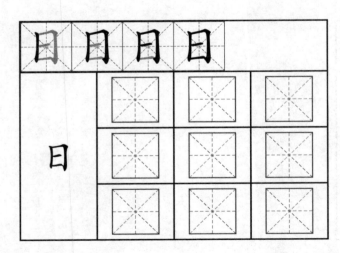

歲／岁 (*suì*)

suì	Ancient Form	Later Form	Modern Traditional Form	Modern Simplified Form
(*measure word for 'years old'*)	歲	歲	歲	岁
Nǐ jǐ suì le?			你幾歲了？	你几岁了？

The ancient form of 歲／岁 (*suì*), the sources tell us, resembled an axe. At harvest time, peasant farmers would use such a tool to gather grain or kill animals for sacrifice. This would normally happen once a year, therefore the character gained the meaning of 'age, time, years.' The modern simplified form, considerably changed, has 山 (*shān*, 'mountain') on the top and 夕 (*xī*, 'sunset') on the bottom. We ran into 夕 'evening' when we learned 多 (*duō*, 'evening on top of evening' > 'numerous'), as our age naturally becomes over time.

你幾歲了？ 　　—我兩歲. 您多大歲數了？ 　　—我七十五了.	你几岁了？ 　　—我两岁. 您多大岁数了？ 　　—我七十五了.

岁 (*suì*) also appears in the following words:

歲數／岁数 age／year + number = 'age'	年歲／年岁 year + age／year = 'age' (Yes, yet another word for 'age'!)

Modern Traditional Form	Modern Simplified Form
歲 歲 歲 歲 歲 歲 歲 歲 歲 歲 歲 歲 歲	岁 岁 岁 岁 岁 岁
歲	岁

生 (shēng)

shēng	Ancient Form	Later Form	Modern Form
be born; give birth	![ancient]	![later]	生
shēngrì			生日

生 (shēng, 'to give birth') pictures, appropriately, a plant sprouting from the ground and is therefore associated with 'birth, life.' The radical 土 (tǔ, 'ground, earth'), a very common radical, can be found within it, almost disguised, but easily 'felt' during writing practice. Write it and feel birth from the 'earth' 土.

Answer the following questions:

• 你是哪年生的? • 你生日是幾月幾號?	• 你是哪年生的? • 你生日是几月几号?

生 also appears in the following words:

生日 birth + day = 'birthday'	生字 birth + character = 'new word'
人生 person + birth = 'life'	出生地 produce + birth + land/place = 'birthplace'

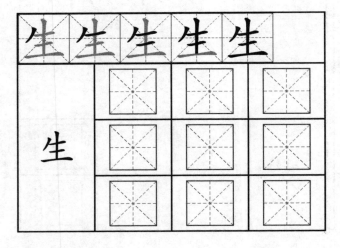

Copyright © 2012 by Yale University and China International Publishing Group

的 (*de*)

de	Ancient Form	Modern Form
(indicates modification)	𣇵	的
wǒ de míngzi		我的名字

We can't say enough about 的 (*de*), a character that, perhaps, is the most important in the language, but for the life of me, I can't find any memory aids. Can you? 的 is the most frequently appearing character among all the thousands in the Chinese language. It signifies 'modification,' one element of language affecting another. Here are some basic examples that should be more or less familiar to you.

• 你的名字 'your name' (lit. name [belonging to] you) • 我的 'mine' (lit. 'of mine'; with noun unexpressed) • 我們的電話號碼. 'Our telephone number.'	• 你的名字 'your name' (lit. name [belonging to] you) • 我的 'mine' (lit. 'of mine'; with noun unexpressed) • 我们的电话号码. 'Our telephone number.'

We will see many other examples of how 的 is used in future lessons of *Encounters*.

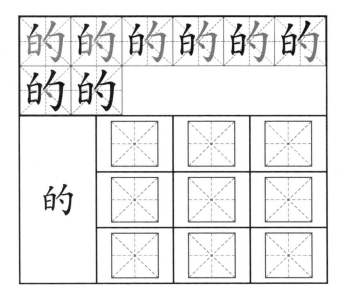

地 (dì)

dì	Ancient Form	Modern Form
land; soil; earth; place	地	地
dìzhǐ		地址

地 (*dì*, 'land; soil; place') has two components, one of which, the right one, you've already seen as the right component in 他 (*tā*). Distinguish 地 and 他. The left part of 地 is 土 (*tǔ*, 'dirt, soil') (slightly altered when part of a compound character; note how both horizontals slant upward). 土 provides a nice link to the meaning 'land, place' and therefore 'address,' but the phonetic 也 (*yě*) offers no pronunciation help at all, and even throws us a curve. This is one where you simply must remember the pronunciation. So, therefore, carefully distinguish 也, 他, 她 (*tā*, 'she'), and 地, all of which are built with 也.

Answer the following question:

你的 e-mail 地址是甚麼?	你的 e-mail 地址是什么?

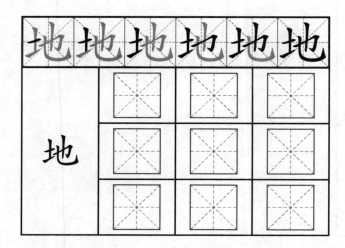

　　　Copyright © 2012 by Yale University and China International Publishing Group

址 (*zhǐ*)

zhǐ	Ancient Form	Later Form	Modern Form
land; earth; place	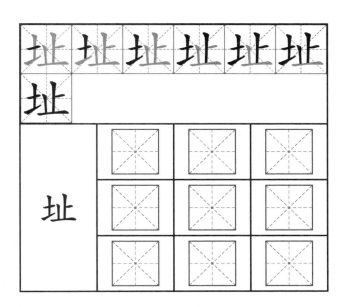	址	址
dìzhǐ			地址

The left part of this character is 土 (*tǔ*, 'land; soil'), an important radical (地, *dì*). On the right is the phonetic or sound component, a reliable one this time. It is 止 (*zhǐ*), meaning 'stop' or 'foot.' So 'soil' under 'foot' is your home, where you 'stop,' your address, your 地址 (*dìzhǐ*).

你的 e-mail 地址是甚麼?　　—地址是 123@abcyahoo.com.　你家的住址是甚麼? (住址, *zhùzhǐ*, 'house address')　　—我的住址是南京路四八二號.	你的 e-mail 地址是什么?　　—地址是 123@abcyahoo.com.　你家的住址是什么? (住址, *zhùzhǐ*, 'house address')　　—我的住址是南京路四八二号.

Note:

地址 (*dìzhǐ*), 'address' (of most anything, including e-mail)

住址 (*zhùzhǐ*), 'address' of where you live (住, *zhù*, 'live, reside')

Unit 3

Get acquainted with the characters of this unit by reading over this list several times. You should be fluent before beginning writing practice. To test yourself, cover the English and see if you can understand the Chinese, and then cover the Chinese and translate the English into Chinese.

时候	時候	time
八点半	八點半	eight thirty (*time*)
今天		today
星期日		Sunday
一分钱	一分錢	one cent
请等我!	請等我!	Please wait for me!
一点钟	一點鍾	one o'clock
晚上		evening
上午		morning; A.M.
下午		afternoon; P.M.
现在	現在	now; at present
有事		have something to do
您早!		Good morning!

Practice with Radicals

Circle the radical of each character below, and link the radical to the meaning of the character. Note that some radicals are characters in themselves with no other components. Examples: 日, 水, 月. One or two characters will be brand new to you. They are actually introduced in the next unit, but try them on for size. Do this exercise before consulting the following page, where the radical of each character is isolated along with its meaning. The number to the upper right of the character references the unit where it is first introduced. And, finally, please note that not all the characters that have been introduced so far are listed here, only those with highly useful radicals.

早[3]	家[4]	你[1]	您[2]	时[3]	晚[3]
位[2]	没[4]	好[1]	地[2]	時[3]	日[2]
说[4]	点[3]	请[1]	国[4]	谢[1]	姓[1]
説[4]	點[3]	請[1]	國[4]	謝[1]	星[3]
过[4]	话[4]	叫[1]	妈[5]		
過[4]	話[4]	侯[3]	媽[5]		

Pinyin	Character	Meaning of Radical	Radical Isolated
dì	地	earth, land, soil	土
diǎn	點/点	fire	火/灬
guò	過/过	road; walk; go	辶
guó	國/国	enclosure/boundary	口
hǎo	好	female/woman	女
hóu	侯	man/person	人/亻
huà	話/话	language/words	言/讠
jiā	家	roof	宀
jiào	叫	mouth	口
mā	媽/妈	female/woman	女
méi	没	water	水/氵
nǐ	你	man/person	人/亻
nín	您	heart, mind	心
qǐng	請/请	language/words	言/讠
rì	日	sun	日
shí	時/时	sun	日
shuō	說/说	language/words	言/讠
wǎn	晚	sun	日
wèi	位	man/person	人/亻
xiè	謝/谢	language/words	言/讠
xīng	星	sun	日
xìng	姓	female/woman	女
zǎo	早	sun	日

上 (shàng)

shàng	Ancient Form	Later Form	Modern Form
above	二	上	上
shàngwǔ			上午

The character 上 (shàng, 'above') can be considered representational, with the horizontal line representing the earth and the upper strokes creating the meaning 'above.' The opposite of 上 is 下 (xià), which is simply 上 upside down!

今天上午見, 好不好?　　　　　　　　 　　—上午不行, 下午好一點兒. 現在幾點了? 　　—上午九點鍾. 早上八點見, 可以 (kěyi, 'may; can; will do') 　　嗎? 　　—可以.	今天上午见, 好不好? 　　—上午不行, 下午好一点儿. 现在几点了? 　　—上午九点钟. 早上八点见, 可以 (kěyi, 'may; can; will do') 　　吗? 　　—可以.

上 also appears in the following words:

上午 upper + noon = 'morning'	早上 (early) morning + upper = (early) 'morning'
上海 up/on + sea = 'Shanghai'	上山 (go) up + mountain = 'go uphill; go mountain climbing'

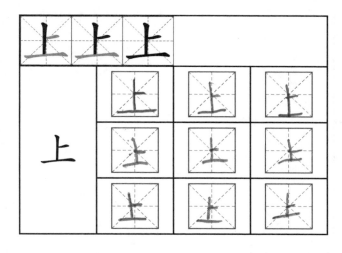

下 (xià)

xià	Ancient Form	Later Form	Modern Form
below; lower	⌒	下	下
xiàwǔ			下午

The character 下 (xià, 'below'), like its 'brother' 上 (shàng, 'above'), can be considered representational, with the horizontal line representing the earth and the lower strokes creating the meaning 'below.' Reread the FYI in your textbook and appreciate how Chinese view time as an 'up and down' concept, 上 ('up') and 下 ('down'), rather than linearly, straight-line-ish. So 'look up' to the morning, 上午 (shàngwǔ), and 'look down' to the afternoon, 下午 (xiàwǔ).

今天上午十點見, 好不好? —不行, 上午没空 (kòng, 'free time'), 有 事, 下午兩點可以. 好, 下午兩點見.	今天上午十点见, 好不好? —不行, 上午没空 (kòng, 'free time'), 有 事, 下午两点可以. 好, 下午两点见.

下 also appears in the following words:

下頭/下头 below + head = 'below; under'	下月 below + month = 'next month'
下半天 lower + half + day = 'afternoon'	下水 (go) down + water = 'be launched (of a boat)'

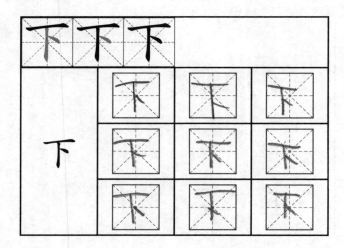

今 (*jīn*)

jīn	Ancient Form	Later Form	Modern Form
today	A	今	今
jīntiān			今天

The ancient form of 今 (*jīn*, 'today') suggests a 'union' with an additional stroke indicating 'contact' (make contact today).

今天星期幾? —今天星期天. 我們今天晚上見, 行不行? —今天晚上不行, 明天吧? 好, 明天見.	今天星期几? —今天星期天. 我们今天晚上见, 行不行? —今天晚上不行, 明天吧? 好, 明天见.

今 also appears in the following words:

今天 today/current + day/heaven = 'today'	今日 today + sun = 'today' (more written than 'spoken')
今生 today/current + live = 'this life'	今年 today/current + year = 'this year'

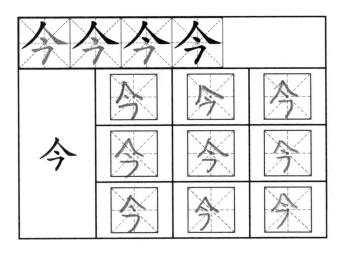

天 (tiān)

tiān	Ancient Form	Later Form	Modern Form
the sky, the heavens; day	𠑹	天	天
jīntiān			今天

The root meaning of 天 (*tiān*) is 'heaven/sky.' Other accounts view it as a person with a big head standing (looking skyward, perhaps?). In the later form, the head flattened to a horizontal line, perhaps again suggesting the sky above. Notice below the top horizontal you can find 大 (*dà*, 'large; great') (heaven is great; today is a great day).

你今天有空嗎? —今天不好, 明天後天 (*hòutiān*, 'the day after tomorrow') 都行. 今天星期幾? —今天星期六, 明天星期天.	你今天有空吗? —今天不好, 明天后天 (*hòutiān*, 'the day after tomorrow') 都行. 今天星期几? —今天星期六, 明天星期天.

天 also appears in the following words and phrases:

我的天哪 (*na*)! 'Good heavens!'	天天 day + day = 'every day; daily'
謝天謝地/谢天谢地 thank + heaven + thank + earth = 'Thank heaven!'	天下 the sky + down/underneath = 'the world; China'

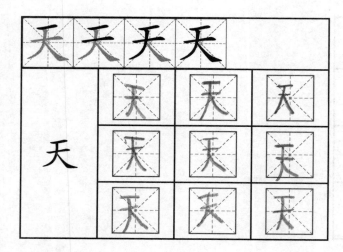

zǎo	Ancient Form	Modern Form
(early) morning	昂	早
Nín zǎo!		您早!

In the character 早 (*zǎo*, '[early] morning'; 'early'), a stative verb, we encounter once again the common radical 日 (*rì*, 'sun'), slightly flattened on top (not as it appears in 時候/时候 *shíhòu*, 'time'). 日 (*rì*), the radical, is on top, 'rising,' 'bright,' as in the morning, above the horizon (the horizontal line below) and going upwards (the vertical line). The sun rising over the horizon is a pretty clear memory aid for 'early morning.'

我們早上八點見, 好不好? 　　—早上八點, 太早了. 九點行不行? 九點不早也不晚. 　　—好, 九點吧.	我们早上八点见, 好不好? 　　—早上八点, 太早了. 九点行不行? 九点不早也不晚. 　　—好, 九点吧.

早 also appears in the following words:

早飯/早饭 morning + meal = 'breakfast'	早上 morning + up/on = 'morning'
早晚 early + late = 'sooner or later'	早點/早点 early + a bit (light) = 'breakfast'

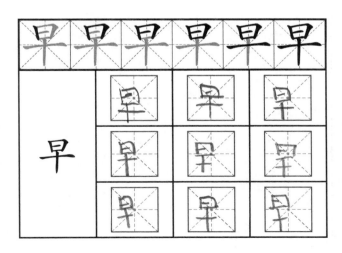

晚 *(wǎn)*

wǎn	Ancient Form	Modern Form
evening; late	晚	晚
wǎnshàng		晚上

晚 (*wǎn*, 'evening; late') is another compound character composed of the by now familiar left part 日 (*rì*, 'sun') as the signific/meaning component, indicating that we're dealing with some aspect of the day, this time the 'evening.' 晚's right part, 免 (*miǎn*), is the phonetic component, but it is reliable only for its vowel (-*an* > *an* > *wan*) part, as is the case with many phonetics. It's interesting that 免 means 'escape,' so, 'escaping from the sun,' and, therefore, 'embracing the cool of the evening.'

今天晚上行不行? —今天晚上, 明天晚上都行. 好, 我們今天晚上七點見.	今天晚上行不行? —今天晚上, 明天晚上都行. 好, 我们今天晚上七点见.

晚 also appears in the following words:

晚安 night + peace = 'good night' (*formal*)	晚會 / 晚会 evening + get together = 'party'
太晚了 'too / very late'	晚飯 / 晚饭 evening + meal = 'supper, dinner'

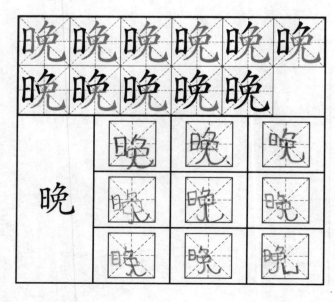

午 (wǔ)

wǔ	Ancient Form	Later Form	Modern Form
noon	8	牛	午
shàngwǔ			上午

午 (*wǔ*, 'noon') is said to be a phonetic loan. It originally meant 'a pestle used to husk rice,' as you might make out from its ancient form. Later it was 'borrowed' to mean 'noon,' and it has kept that meaning since ancient times. The character 午 combines with 上 (*shàng*, 'up/before') and 下 (*xià*, 'down/after') to form the meanings '(late) morning' 上午 (*shàngwǔ*) and 'afternoon' 下午 (*xiàwǔ*).

上午十點半見. 　—不行, 上午有事. 下午四點, 可以嗎? 可以. 下午四點見. 　—好. 不見不散. (*bú jiàn bú sàn*,* 'not see not go/disperse' > 'Don't leave before I get there!')	上午十点半见. 　—不行, 上午有事. 下午四点, 可以吗? 可以. 下午四点见. 　—好. 不见不散. (*bú jiàn bú sàn*,* 'not see not go/disperse' > 'Don't leave before I get there!')

*A typical Chinese four-character phrase said upon concluding an agreement to meet at a certain time.

午 also appears in the following words:

午飯 / 午饭 noon + meal = 'lunch'	中午 middle + noon = 'noon'
下午 below + noon = 'afternoon'	上午 up + noon = 'morning'

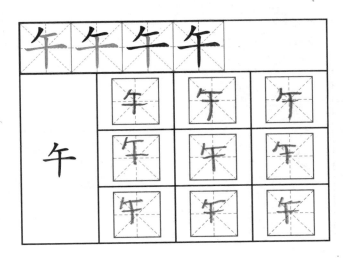

現／现 (*xiàn*)

xiàn	Ancient Form	Modern Traditional Form	Modern Simplified Form
now; at present	現	現	现
xiànzài		現在	现在

現／现 (*xiàn*, 'now; at present') is a typical component character, with the radical on the left (王 *wáng*, 'king') and the now familiar 见 *jiàn* (cf. 再见) on the right. Memory aid: the guidance of the 'king' can brighten the present).

現在幾點鐘? —現在上午九點半. 你現在有空嗎? —有, 有, 有.	现在几点钟? —现在上午九点半. 你现在有空吗? —有, 有, 有.

現／现 also appears in the following words:

現今／现今 present + now = 'the present age'	現在／现在 now, at present + be in, at = 'the present; now; nowadays'
現金／现金 now; at present + money = 'ready cash'	現有／现有 now + have = 'have on hand'

Modern Traditional Form	Modern Simplified Form
現 現 現 現 現 現 現 現 現 現 現	现 现 现 现 现 现 现 现

在 (zài)

zài	Ancient Form	Later Form	Modern Form
at; exist	屮	扗	在
xiànzài			現在 / 现在

The character 在 (zài) has many meanings, several of which we will learn in future encounters with 在. Relevant for us is its use in the compound 現在/现在 (xiànzài, 'now'). Notice the radical 土 (tǔ, 'earth, land') (seen also in 地址 dìzhǐ, 'address'). The ancient form is a picture of grass coming from the earth, and thus existing 'in the here and now.'

• 現在幾點了? 現在六點半.	• 现在几点了? 现在六点半.
• 現在不行, 明天後天都可以.	• 现在不行, 明天后天都可以.
• 他現在怎麼樣? 還好.	• 他现在怎么样? 还好.
• 現在有空嗎? 對不起, 剛才有空, 現在有點兒事. (空, kòng, 'free time')	• 现在有空吗? 对不起, 刚才有空, 现在有点儿事。(空, kòng, 'free time')

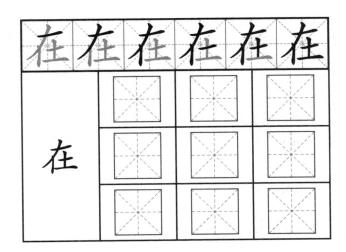

半 (bàn)

bàn	Ancient Form	Modern Form
half	半	半
bā diǎn bàn		八點半 / 八点半

半 (*bàn*, 'half') can be thought of as representational. Notice how the vertical stroke cuts the character in half; notice on top how an 'upside down' 八 (*bā*, 'eight'), which also in ancient times meant 'to divide', splits a 牛 (*niú*, 'cow') in 'half,' right there in the character. Can you make out a 牛 in this character?

我們九點半見, 好不好? 　—太早, 太早, 十一點半, 可以嗎? 好, 上午十一點半見!	我们九点半见, 好不好? 　—太早, 太早, 十一点半, 可以吗? 好, 上午十一点半见!

半 (*bàn*) also appears in the following words and phrases:

多半 more + half = 'more than half'	半天 half + day = 'a long time'
一半 one + half = 'half; one-half'	兩個半鍾頭 / 两个半钟头 two + *ge* + half + hour = 'two and a half hours'

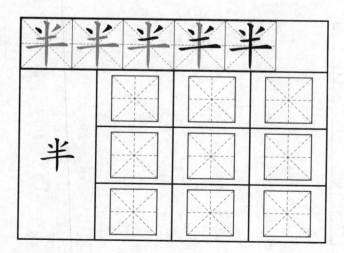

分 (fēn)

fēn	Ancient Form	Modern Form
minute (*of time*); cent, penny	川	分
yì fēn qián		一分錢 / 一分钱

分 (*fēn*) 'minute' (of time) or 'particle' of money—therefore, 'cent'—is an interesting 'top-bottom' compound character composed of 'eight' on top and 刀 (*dāo*, 'knife') below. Think of a knife dividing up a dollar into cents or cutting an hour into minutes; after all, the primary meaning of 分 is 'to divide.'

八點四十分	五點過五分	早上四點鐘
八点四十分	五点过五分	早上四点钟

Observe below how 分(*fēn*) serves as a reliable phonetic (except for tones) in some common characters that you will learn in the future. The point here for learners is to reinforce further an appreciation of the role of phonetics in guessing the pronunciation of characters newly encountered, an important learning strategy. Such a skill can shortcut dictionary lookups; it can perhaps recall to you a word you know in your spoken language inventory but whose pronunciation you've forgotten. Put simply, radicals help with meaning; phonetics help with pronunciation, and, with Chinese, we need all the help we can muster.

份 (*fèn*)	粉 (*fěn*)	纷 (*fēn*)	吩 (*fēn*)	忿 (*fèn*)
part; portion; share (*with 'man' radical*)	noodles; powder (*with 'rice' radical*)	disorderly (*with 'silk' radical*)	tell, instruct, command (*with 'mouth' radical*)	angry; indignant (*with 'heart' radical*)

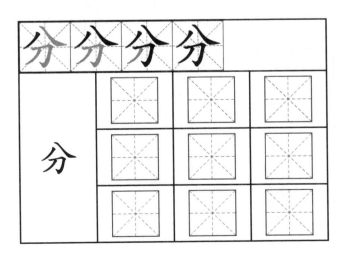

點／点 (*diǎn*)

diǎn	Ancient Form	Modern Traditional Form	Modern Simplifed Form
a dot, a spot, a bit; hour (*on the clock*)	點	點	点
yì diǎn zhōng		一點鐘	一点钟

點／点 (*diǎn*) originally meant 'small black dot(s),' which are quite visible in both modern forms at the bottom of the character. The four dots, by the way, are the combining form of the radical 火 (*huǒ*, 'fire'). Remember 火 from the introductory unit? 'Small black dots,' licks of flame, has led to modern meanings such as 'a small amount, a bit, a little' (一點／一点, *yì diǎn*), all the way to 'a small amount of time' or 'a point on the clock'—therefore, 'hour' of the day.

Count off the hours of the day:
一點鐘, 兩點鐘, 三點鐘, 十二點鐘／一点钟, 两点钟, 三点钟, 十二点钟

Review some 'off the hour' expressions:
四點半 (鐘), 五點一刻 (鐘) ／四点半 (钟), 五点一刻 (钟)

點／点 also appears in the following words:

點鐘／点钟 dot + clock = 'time' (on the clock)	點心／点心 a bit + heart = 'dessert; pastries'
點火／点火 to ignite + fire = 'light a fire; stir up trouble'	一點／一点 one + dot = 'a little of something' (often with 兒／儿 suffix)

Modern Traditional Form	Modern Simplified Form
點 點 點 點 點 點 點 點 點 點 點 點 點 點 點 點 點	点 点 点 点 点 点 点 点 点
點	点

星 (*xīng*)

xīng	Ancient Form	Later Form	Modern Form
star; week	𣇪	曐	星
xīngqīsān			星期三

星 (*xīng*, 'star; week') is a compound character composed of 日 (*rì*, 'sun') (on top), giving 'birth' 生 (*shēng*) to 'stars,' many stars in the ancient form. 生 (*shēng*, 'birth') originally functioned as the phonetic component, which was likely reliable way back then, but after centuries of language change is not quite so reliable anymore.

Review the days of week: 星期一 to 星期六, but don't forget 星期天 or 星期日 for Sunday!

今天星期幾? 　—星期三. 不是吧! 　—哦, 對了, 不是星期三, 是星期二.	今天星期几? 　—星期三. 不是吧! 　—哦, 对了, 不是星期三, 是星期二.

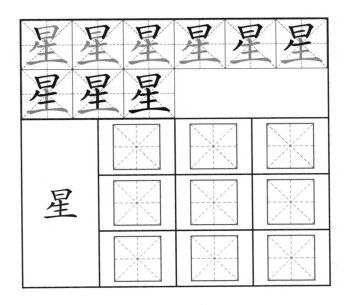

期 (*qī*)

qī	Ancient Form	Modern Form
time period; term	舼	期
xīngqī		星期

期 (*qī*, 'time period; term') presents the 月 (*yuè*, 'moon') radical on the right with a left-side phonetic 其 (*qí*). Memory aid: the 'moon' reminds us of the Chinese lunar calendar composed of months (月) and weeks (星期, *xīngqī*). Recall that Chinese has two words for 'week' and 'days of the week,' one formed with 星期 and the other with 禮拜/礼拜 (*lǐbài*). Try saying the days of the week, Monday through Sunday, with both forms, keeping in mind that the Chinese week begins with Monday.

七月四號是星期幾? 　—是星期日. 你星期日有空嗎? 　—有, 有, 有.	七月四号是星期几? 　—是星期日. 你星期日有空吗? 　—有, 有, 有.

期	期	期	期	期	期
期	期	期	期	期	期

期

時/时 (*shí*)

shí	Ancient Form	Modern Traditional Form	Modern Simplified Form
(point in) time	𣇈	時	时
shíhòu		時候	时候

時/时 (*shí*, [point in] 'time') combines a radical we've seen before and will see many times again—日 (*rì*, 'sun') (time is measured by the sun)—with the phonetic 寺 (*sì*, 'temple') on the right (time is in the hands of the gods). The simplified graph replaces the phonetic with a different character, actually 'inch' (寸, *cùn*) (an inch of time?).

我們甚麼時候見? 　　—上午十點, 行不行? 不行. 　　—十一點, 可以不可以? (可以, *kěyi*, 　　　'may; can; will do') 可以. 不見不散. (*bú jiàn bú sàn*)	我们什么时候见? 　　—上午十点, 行不行? 不行. 　　—十一点, 可以不可以? (可以, *kěyi*, 　　　'may; can; will do') 可以. 不见不散. (*bú jiàn bú sàn*)

時/时 also appears in the following words:

小時/小时 small + time = 'hour'	有時/有时 have + time= 'sometimes'
時間/时间 time + among, between = 'time' 　(period)	小時候/小时候 young + time = 'during 　one's youth'

Modern Traditional Form	Modern Simplified Form
時 時 時 時 時 時 時 時 時 時	时 时 时 时 时 时 时
時	时

候 (hòu)

hòu	Ancient Form	Modern Form
time; moment	候	候
shíhòu		時候 / 时候

候 (hòu, 'time') is a compound of 'person' on the left (亻 , as a 'standing man') and 㑑 (hóu) on the right, the phonetic component (less one stroke). One interpretation of the ancient meaning takes it as a 'person shooting an arrow at a target,' 'waiting on time' for the arrow to hit its mark. That fits our purposes very well here, since we are all waiting on 'time.' Another? 'Time waits for no man.'

我們甚麼時候見? 　—兩點半, 可以嗎? 好. 不見不散.	我们什么时候见? 　—两点半, 可以吗? 好. 不见不散.

Copyright © 2012 by Yale University and China International Publishing Group

等 (děng)

děng	Ancient Form	Modern Form
wait; wait for	等	等
Qǐng nǐ děng wǒ.		請你等我 / 请你等我

等 (*děng*, 'wait') takes the radical 'bamboo' 竹 (*zhú*), which is altered to ⺮ when it forms the top part of a compound character, as in 等. Long ago, it is said, people in China wrote messages on bamboo slips and deposited them in temples, waiting for a response from the gods.

• 等一等.	• 等一等.
• 請您等我, 好不好?	• 请您等我, 好不好?
• 等半個鍾頭.	• 等半个钟头.
• 謝謝你等我.	• 谢谢你等我.

等等等等等等
等等等等等等

等

有 (yǒu)

yǒu	Ancient Form	Later Form	Modern Form
have; possess			有
méiyǒu			没有

有 (*yǒu*, 'have, possess') is a a compound of 'hand,' the top part (seen perhaps more easily in the later form), and the 月 (*yuè*, 'moon') radical. Perhaps we can take it as the hand of mankind reaching out to possess the abundance of the moon—a stretch, perhaps, but it's all I've got right now. Keep in mind that 有 is unique among verbs in Chinese in that it is negated by 没 (*méi*) and only 没, never with 不 (*bù*).

你明天有没有空? 　　—對不起, 没有空, 有很多事. 後天可以嗎? (後天, *hòutiān*, 'the day after 　　tomorrow') 　　—不行, 後天也有事.	你明天有没有空? 　　—对不起, 没有空, 有很多事. 后天可以吗? (后天, *hòutiān*, 'the day after 　　tomorrow') 　　—不行, 后天也有事.

有 also appears in the following words:

有名 have + name = 'well-known; famous'	有的人 have + *de* + person = 'some people'
有事 have + matter, affair = 'busy; occupied'	没有 no + have = 'be without; not have'

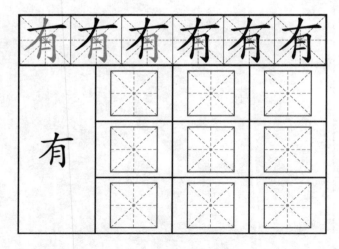

事 (*shì*)

shì	Ancient Form	Later Form	Modern Form
affair; matter	✲	事	事
yǒu shì			有事

Take an extra careful look at the character 事 (*shì*, 'affair; matter')—unlike others, it is not easily analyzed into the usual two side-by-side or up-and- down constructs that you've seen before. Moreover, it is not representational like 山 (*shān*, 'mountain'), 日 (*rì*, 'sun'), or 月 (*yuè*, 'moon'), all of which, with a little imagining, resemble what they mean. So 事 might give you a bit of trouble, take a bit more effort, and that's what this character is all about, something troublesome, a job, some 'busy-ness,' some matter that interrupts your usual routine. And, when writing, take the trouble to make sure the last stroke is the vertical that descends through the entire character.

現在幾點了? —早上六點. 甚麼事? 對不起, 對不起, 沒事, 沒事.	现在几点了? —早上六点. 什么事? 对不起, 对不起, 没事, 没事.

事 also appears in the following words:

小事 small, minor + affair= 'a trifle'	有事 have + affair = 'busy; have something to do'
大事 great, important + affair = 'something significant/important'	一件事 one + *jiàn* (*measure*) + affair = 'a matter, piece of business'

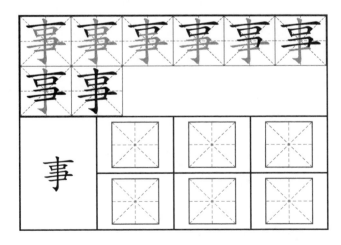

Unit 4

Get acquainted with the characters of this unit by reading over this list several times. You should be fluent before beginning writing practice. To test yourself, cover the English and see if you can understand the Chinese, and then cover the Chinese and translate the English into Chinese.

喜欢	喜歡	like; prefer
没去		didn't go
去过	去過	have gone to
会说	會説	able to speak
说话	説話	say; speak
中国	中國	China
英国	英國	England
美国	美國	America; the U.S.
我家		my home
出生		to be born
说得好!	説得好!	Said well!
中文		Chinese
都懂		understand (it) all

Five Useful Phonetics

This manual has made quite a point about phonetics, trying to persuade you how they can help you with recall of pronunciation of Chinese characters. Below we give you five useful phonetics. Go through this exercise and see how phonetics come in handy.

Let's be certain: we're not trying to teach you the new characters listed below, some of which you will not meet for a long time, and some others, perhaps never (like 'cyanic acid'). Our point: phonetics can help.

Knowing the 馬/马 (*mǎ*) phonetic can help you pronounce or recall the pronunciation of the following characters:

嗎/吗	媽/妈	碼/码	螞/蚂	罵/骂
ma	*mā*	*mǎ*	*mǎ*	*mà*
(*question particle*)	mom	number (*page, etc.*)	ant	curse; swear

Knowing the 青 (*qīng*) phonetic can help with the following characters:

請/请	情	晴	清	鯖	氰
qǐng	*qíng*	*qíng*	*qīng*	*qīng*	*qíng*
request; invite	sentiment; feeling	clear (*of weather*)	clear (*of liquids*)	mackerel	cyanic acid

Knowing the 門/门 (*mén*) phonetic can help with:

門/门	們/们	悶/闷	悶/闷	焖
mén	*men*	*mèn*	*mēn*	*mèn*
door	(*plural suffix*)	bored; depressed	stuffy; close	boil; braise

(Notice with 悶/闷 above that sometimes one character with the same shape but different tone can sometimes serve two meanings.)

Knowing the 巴 (*bā*) phonetic can help with:

爸	把	吧	爬	疤	耙
bà	*bǎ*	*ba*	*pá*	*bā*	*pá*
dad	hold	(*suggestion particle*); grasp	climb	scar	rake

Knowing the 分 (*fēn*) phonetic can help with:

忿	份	粉	吩	紛/纷
fèn	*fèn*	*fěn*	*fēn*	*fēn*
anger; wrath	share; portion	noodles	tell; instruct	confused; disorderly

These five phonetics (not the new characters) are all drawn from characters you have learned or will learn in the first five units. They are all rather reliable. As we've said before, phonetics, as a rule, are not as reliable as the ones shown above, but they all can help in one way or another. The Chinese people use them for recall purposes, why not us?

As an additional exercise, look over the above characters and see how many radicals you can identify.

中 (*zhōng*)

zhōng	Ancient Form	Later Form	Modern Form
middle; central; China	屮	中	中
Zhōngguó			中國 / 国

中 (*zhōng*, 'China') offers some obvious clues. A vertical line descends through the middle of a box or enclosure, splitting it in half. The Chinese have for centuries believed that their country stands at the middle of the world, calling it 'Central Kingdom.' Given China's recent history, there is increasingly powerful proof of this age-old tradition of China playing a central role in the world.

你是日本人嗎? 　—不, 不, 我不日本人, 我是中國人. 你是中國哪兒的人? 　—我是中國北京人.	你是日本人吗? 　—不, 不, 我不日本人, 我是中国人. 你是中国哪儿的人? 　—我是中国北京人.

中 also appears in the following words:

中美 China + U.S. = 'Sino-American'	中文 Chinese + language = (written) 'Chinese'
中國 / 中国 middle + country = 'China'	地中海 land + middle + sea = 'Mediterranean Sea'

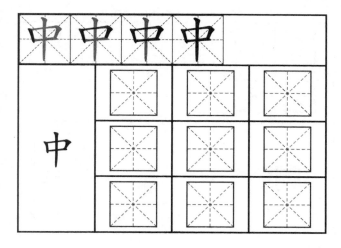

國/国 (*guó*)

guó	Ancient Form	Later Form	Modern Traditional Form	Modern Simplified Form
country; nation; state	可	國	國	国
Zhōngguó			中國	中国

Perhaps the most useful memory association for the character 國/国 (*guó*, 'nation; country') is the surrounding frame representing the boundaries of a country. The simplification process has replaced the inside 或 (*huò*) (which serves as the traditional character phonetic: *huò > huò > huò > guó*) with 玉 (*yù*, 'jade'), the precious stone so highly valued by the 'nation' of China. What do you think of the simplification?

中國	中國人	中國話	中国	中国人	中国话
美國	美國人	美國話	美国	美国人	美国话
德國	德國人	德國話	德国	德国人	德国话
英國	英國人	英國話	英国	英国人	英国话
法國	法國人	法國話	法国	法国人	法国话
韓國	韓國人	韓國話	韩国	韩国人	韩国话

國/国 also appears in the following words:

大國/大国 large, great + country = 'a great/important nation/country'	國人/国人 country + person/people = 'countrymen'
出國/出国 out + country = 'go abroad'	國文/国文 nation + language = (written) 'Chinese'

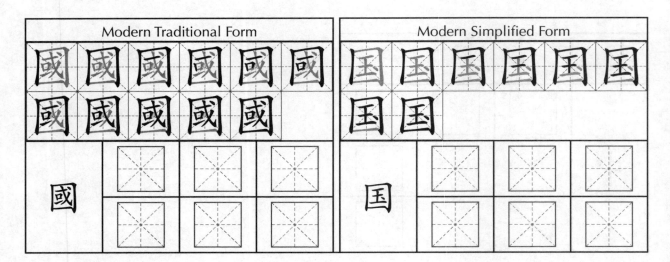

家 (*jiā*)

jiā	Ancient Form	Later Form	Modern Form
family; home	𠖾	家	家
wǒ jiā			我家

家 (*jiā*) is a fun character, containing some valuable culturally based information. The top, a common radical, is 'roof' (of a home). Now what's important to the economic health of a family in China (or elsewhere, for that matter)? Why, a pig, of course, and that's what we see underneath the roof. Any 'family'—any 'household'— needs a pig, reminding us that China was, and still is, an agriculturally based, family-oriented society. Of course, it is changing, and rapidly so.

你家在哪兒? 　　—我家在北京. 你家呢? 我家在上海.	你家在哪儿? 　　—我家在北京. 你家呢? 我家在上海.

家 also appears in the following words:

我家 me/mine + home = 'my family/home' [Notice: no 的 (*de*) required, although some speakers will include it.]	家人 home + person = 'family members'
大家 big + family = 'everyone'	國家/国家 nation + home = 'country'

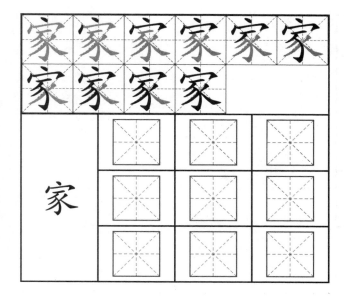

měi	Ancient Form	Later Form	Modern Form
beautiful; (America)	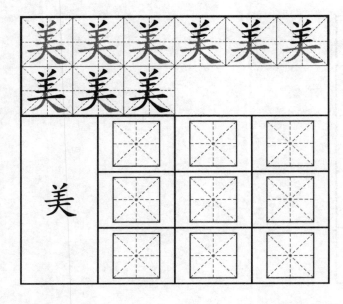		美
Měiguó			美國 / 美国

The root meaning of 美 (*měi*) is 'beautiful,' like the figure of a person (大) with a beautiful feathered headdress. Relevant for us here is when 美 combines with 國/国 (*guó*) to mean 'A-mei-ri-ka' (transliteration)—'America, the beautiful,' the United States. Look closely and notice 大 (*dà*) at the bottom, 'the great American' continent.

你是美國人嗎? 　　—是, 我是美國人. 我家在紐約. 你去過 　　　美國嗎? (紐約, *Niǔyuē*, 'New York') 没去過, 很想去.	你是美国人吗? 　　—是, 我是美国人. 我家在纽约. 你去过 　　　美国吗? (纽约, *Niǔyuē*, 'New York') 没去过, 很想去.

美 also appears in the following words:

美人 beautiful + person = 'a beautiful woman	美元 American + dollar = 'U.S. dollar/ currency'
美好 beautiful + good = 'fine; happy'	中美 China + U.S. = 'Sino-American' (relations, etc.)

英 (*yīng*)

yīng	Ancient Form	Modern Form
heroic; (England; Britain)	㑒	英
Yīngguó		英國 / 英国

英 (*yīng*, 'England') is a prototypical radical plus phonetic character, with the radical 艹 'plant' (notice the alteration of 艸 when it combines as a top radical). The bottom part, 央 (*yāng*), is the phonetic component. How did the character come to be associated with 'England'? Here's where transliteration and the phonetic 央 comes into play. 央 is similar to the first syllable of Ingland/England (think of 'Yingland'). Thus the Chinese found a way to express the name of the country that played such a part in their history. Compare: Ah-mei-ri-ka, 美國 / 美国 (*Měiguó*), and several others in this lesson.

英國　英國人　英文	英国　英国人　英文
你會说英文嗎? 　　—不會, 可是 (*kěshì*, 'but') 很想學一點兒.	你会说英文吗? 　　—不会, 可是 (*kěshì*, 'but') 很想学一点儿.

Review the names of countries: supply the Chinese equivalents of the following: Germany, Russia, France, Spain, England, Italy, China, Japan, India, Korea.

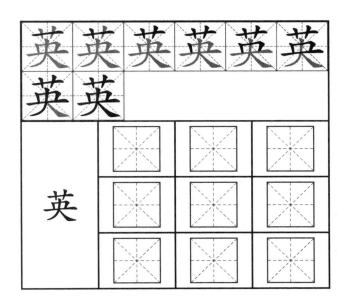

文 (wén)

wén	Ancient Form	Later Form	Modern Form
language; (written) language	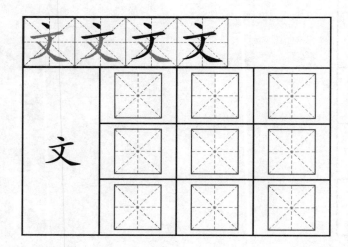		文
Zhōngwén			中文

You've actually seen the 文 (*wén*) character before. In Unit 2 it was a component of the simplified character 這/这 (*zhè/zhèi*, 'this'). Make sure to distinguish the two: 這/这 vs. 文. 文 originally meant tatooing on the skin, making symbols on the skin, and, by extension, 'making symbols on paper,' and therefore came into its modern meaning of 'writing.' 文 combines easily with names of countries to create names of languages. Let's review them here. Can you identify all of them?

Asian languages: 中文, 日文, 韓文, 印度 (*Yìndu*, 'India') 文
European languages: 英文, 法文, 德文, 俄文, 西班牙文

Names of countries also combine with 話/话 (*huà*) to form names of languages, so 中國話/中国话 (*Zhōngguó huà*), 日本話/日本话 (*Rìběn huà*), and so on. Name a few more.

文 文 文 文

文

xǐ	Ancient Form	Later Form	Modern Form
like; prefer	🎵	喜	喜
xǐhuān			喜歡 / 喜欢

喜 (xǐ) combines a 'drum' on the top and a 口 (kǒu, 'mouth') on the bottom. How then do we reach the meaning 'to like/prefer'? We do express our 'preferences' orally, right? So, therefore, the 口 at the bottom. Perhaps you can provide a better memory aid. Share your ideas for memory aids with your classmates. And, remember 喜 is followed by 歡/欢 (huān), making 喜歡 / 喜欢 (xǐhuān).

你喜歡旅行嗎? (Nǐ xǐhuān lǚxíng ma?) —很不喜歡旅行. (lǚxíng, 'travel') 我只喜歡呆 (dāi, 'stay') 在家裡. 哪兒都不想去。	你喜欢旅行吗? (Nǐ xǐhuān lǚxíng ma?) —很不喜欢旅行. (lǚxíng, 'travel') 我只喜欢呆 (dāi, 'stay') 在家里. 哪儿都不想去。

喜	喜	喜	喜	喜	喜
喜	喜	喜	喜	喜	喜

喜			

歡/欢 (huān)

huān	Ancient Form	Modern Traditional Form	Modern Simplified Form
happy; joyful	歡	歡	欢
xǐhuān		喜歡	喜欢

The character 欢 (huān, 'happy') does not easily suggest a memory aid, unless you can imagine the right side as a person (人, rén [the lower part]) smiling (upper right part). The relevant vocabulary connection for us is 喜歡/喜欢 (xǐhuān, 'to prefer; to like'). When you get what you prefer, you're usually 'happy.' Another view of this character is to regard the right side as a 'singing person' who is happy that he got his preference. Can you suggest another memory prompt? Talk it over with your classmates.

• 你喜歡旅行嗎?
—不喜歡. 我喜歡呆在家裡.
• 那個學生很喜歡説中國話.

• 你喜欢旅行吗?
—不喜欢. 我喜欢呆在家里.
• 那个学生很喜欢说中国话.

Modern Traditional Form	Modern Simplified Form
歡 歡	欢 欢 欢 欢 欢 欢
歡	欢

説/说 (*shuō*)

shuō	Ancient Form	Modern Traditional Form	Modern Simplified Form
speak; say; talk	說	説	说
shuōhuà		説話	说话

説/说 (*shuō*) shows the now familiar left-side radical 言/讠 (speech), which gives a clue to its meaning. You've seen 言/讠 before in 請/请 (*qǐng*) and 謝/谢 (*xiè*), both of which suggest actions involving speaking. Some analysts regard the right side (兑) as contributing to meaning as well, suggesting it resembles a 'person,' a slightly altered 人 (*rén*) at the bottom; therefore, a person speaking. 説/说 combines nicely with 話/话 (*huà*, 'language/words') to render the verb-object 説話/说话 (*shuōhuà*).

您會説俄語嗎? (語, *yǔ*, 'language') 　—只會説一點兒, 説得不好. 您太客氣, 説得很好. (客氣, *kèqi*, 'polite')	您会说俄语吗? (语, *yǔ*, 'language') 　—只会说一点儿, 说得不好. 您太客气, 说得很好. (客气, *kèqi*, 'polite')

説/说 also appears in the following words:

説法/说法 talk + way = 'view; way of speaking' (法, also 'France')	説明/说明 talk + clear = 'explain'
会説/会说 able to + speak = 'able to speak' (foreign languages, etc.)	小説/小说 small/minor + talk = 'fiction; a novel'

Modern Traditional Form	Modern Simplified Form
説 説 説 説 説 説 説 説 説 説 説 説 説 説	说 说 说 说 说 说 说 说 说
説	说

話/话 (*huà*)

huà	Ancient Form	Modern Traditional Form	Modern Simplified Form
(spoken) words; speech; language	話	話	话
shuōhuà		説話	说话

話/话 (*huà*) is a character with more than one association. As one would expect, the radical is 言 (*yán*, 'speech') on the left (simplified form, 讠), so that's the link to the meaning 'words.' Another link, less useful perhaps, is the right part, 舌 (*shé*, 'tongue'), also a requirement for the act of 'speaking.'

• 他是法國人, 可是不會說法國話.	• 他是法国人, 可是不会说法国话.
• 你會說俄國話嗎?	• 你会说俄国话吗?
—只會說一點兒俄國話.	—只会说一点儿俄国话.
• 他說中國話, 說得很好.	• 他说中国话, 说得很好.

話/话 also appears in the following words:

對話/对话 facing + speech = 'dialogue'	説話/说话 to talk + speech = 'to talk; speak'
好話/好话 good + words = 'fine-sounding language'	大話/大话 large/big + words = 'boastful talk'

Modern Traditional Form	Modern Simplified Form
話 話 話 話 話 話 話 話 話 話 話 話 話	话 话 话 话 话 话 话 话
話	话

會/会 *(huì)*

huì	Ancient Form	Later Form	Modern Traditional Form	Modern Simplified Form
will; can; able to			會	会
Wǒ huì shuō Zhōngwén.			我會说中文.	我会说中文.

會/会 *(huì)* has several meanings. Relevant for us are two in particular: 'will' (indicating future intent or possibility) and 'can' (indicating learned ability). It's not easy to come up with a memory aid for this character. Can you suggest something?

你今年想去甚麼地方?	你今年想去什么地方?
——我今年很想去中國, 也會去非洲.	——我今年很想去中国, 也会去非洲.
你會说中國話嗎?	你会说中国话吗?
——會说一點兒, 可是说得不好.	——会说一点儿, 可是说得不好.
你太客氣! 你说得很好.	你太客气! 你说得很好.

Modern Traditional Form	Modern Simplified Form

dōu	Ancient Form	Modern Form
all	𦧌	都
Wǒmen dōu hǎo!		我們都好! / 我们都好!

The character 都 (*dōu*, 'all') originally meant 'city; capital' (that's the meaning of its right-side radical), thus linking it to its modern meaning—'all' the people in town; therefore, 'all; everybody; both.'

• 你都在哪裡住過? (呆, *dāi*, 'stay') 　　—很多地方. 中國, 日本, 韓國, 我都住過. • 你們都好嗎? 　　—我們都很好, 謝謝.	• 你都在哪里住过? (呆, *dāi*, 'stay') 　　—很多地方. 中国, 日本, 韩国, 我都住过. • 你们都好吗? 　　—我们都很好, 谢谢.

都 都 都 都 都 都
都 都 都 都 都

都

得 (de)

de	Ancient Form	Modern Form
(adverb of manner particle)	得	得
Shuō de hěn hǎo!		説得很好! / 说得很好!

得 (*de*), for our purposes in Unit 4, performs a grammar function. 得 is appended to verbs in a grammar pattern that expesses 'how' one does a certain action. For example, speaking a foreign language. Do you speak it well? Then 説 / 说得很好. Not well? Then, 説 / 说得不好, and so on, with many verbal actions. Like most grammar function words, 得 is neutral in tone. Toned 得 (*dé*) means 'to get; to acquire.' So we might remember 得 (*de*) as an indicator of 'achieving' a certain level of attainment (or not!)

But that's not the whole story of 得. When pronounced *děi* with the third tone, the same character takes on a new meaning: 'must.' Example: 對不起, 我得走了, 再見! / 对不起, 我得走了, 再见! ('Sorry, but I must go now, so long!') With some characters, if you change the tone (and, sometimes, the pronunciation as well), you change the meaning. 得 illustrates that point nicely.

你會説日文嗎? 　—會説一點兒, 可是説得不好. 您太客氣. 你一定説得很好. (一定 *yídìng* 　'certainly')	你会说日文吗? 　—会说一点儿, 可是说得不好. 您太客气. 你一定说得很好. (一定 *yídìng* 　'certainly')

得 pronounced with the second tone (*dé*) means 'get; attain.' Here's a bonus phrase involving 得: 一舉兩得 / 一举两得 (*yījǔ liǎngdé*, 'One move, two gains' > 'Kill two birds with one stone.')

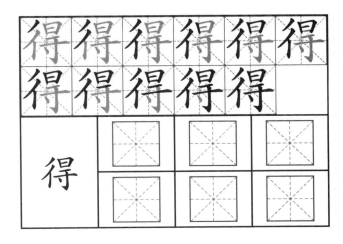

没 (méi)

méi	Ancient Form	Later Form	Modern Form
not have; be without	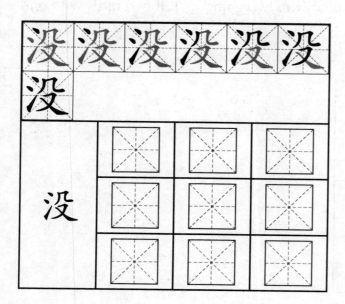		没
méiyǒu			没有

The clue for the character 没 (*méi*) is the left-side water radical, which is 氵 (*shuǐ*) when a radical, but 水 (*shuǐ*) when a full form character. We ran into 水 in the introductory unit. 水 combines with the right side to create the meaning 'sink in the water,' made pretty obvious in the early forms. Thus we arrive at our relevant meaning, from 'sink to nowhere, to nothingness' to 'not being,' 'being without'; so, 没有 (*méiyǒu*).

你去過中國嗎? 　—沒 (有) 去過. 你有中文姓嗎? 　—沒有. 很想有.	你去过中国吗? 　—没 (有) 去过. 你有中文姓吗? 　—没有. 很想有.

没 没 没 没 没 没

没

去 (qù)

qù	Ancient Form	Later Form	Modern Form
to go	去	去	去
qù Zhōngguó			去中国

去 (qù, 'go') is a character whose ancient forms may be of some memory aid. Some see the top part as resembling a person and the bottom a cave, and envision a 'person going out of a cave.' 去, a character with very few strokes, can pose a particular problem for memory hounds like us. And that is, the fewer strokes a character has, the harder it is to form memory aids. Of course, there are the obvious exceptions of 一, 二, and 三, and some really 'picture-perfect' characters like 山 (shān), 水 (shuǐ), 月 (yuè), and others. So remembering fewer-stroke characters might take some extra effort. Always remember that context is your constant friend for comprehension.

我很想去中國. 你也想去嗎? 　—很想去. 你想甚麼時候去? 我想明年去.	我很想去中国. 你也想去吗? 　—很想去. 你想什么时候去? 我想明年去.

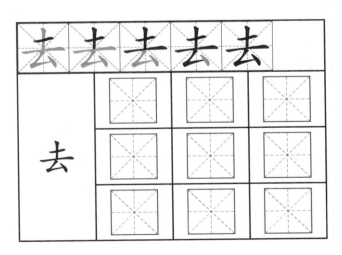

過/过 (guò)

guò	Ancient Form	Modern Traditional Form	Modern Simplified Form
(verb suffix to indicate experience)	過	過	过
qùguo Zhōngguó		去過中國	去过中国

過/过 (guò) is another grammatical function word, a verbal suffix. 過/过 is suffixed to many action verbs to express having experienced or not experienced the verbal action. So, 住過/住过 (zhùguo, 'have lived [in a certain place in the past]). 過/过 literally means 'to pass,' thus the link to the meaning 'to come to pass, to have experienced.' Note how the character has been considerably modified in the change from traditional to simplified, but it has retained the left-side radical 辶, which means 'to walk; go' (seen previously in 這/这, zhèi/zhè, 'this').

你去過中國嗎?   ——去過.   日本呢?   ——日本沒去過. 很想去.

你去过中国吗?   ——去过.   日本呢?   ——日本没去过. 很想去.

Modern Traditional Form
過 過 過 過 過 過
過 過 過 過 過 過
過

過

Modern Simplified Form
过 过 过 过 过 过

过

出 (*chū*)

chū	Ancient Form	Later Form	Modern Form
produce; come out	![ancient form]	![later form]	出
chūshēng			出生

出 (*chū*, 'produce') is a pictograph of a sprouting plant, thus its association with 'produce; issue forth; come out,' and so on. Some view the top part as a foot and the bottom part as the gate of a cave. The character, some say, looks like a foot coming forth from a cave. What do you see?

你是在哪兒出生的? 　—我是在法國出生的. 你呢? 我是在美國出生, 也在美國長大的.	你是在哪儿出生的? 　—我是在法国出生的. 你呢? 我是在美国出生, 也在美国长大的.

出 also appears in the following words:

日出 sun + come out = 'sunrise'	出口 come out + mouth = 'export'
出名 produce + name = 'famous/well-known'	出生 produce + give birth = 'be born'

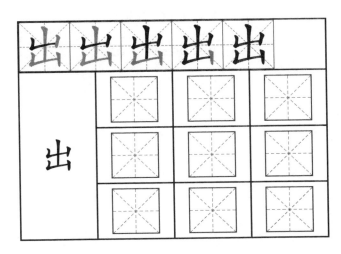

Unit 5

Get acquainted with the characters of this unit by reading over this list several times. You should be fluent before beginning writing practice. To test yourself, cover the English and see if you can understand the Chinese, and then cover the Chinese and translate the English into Chinese.

父亲	父親	father
兄弟		brothers
男朋友		boyfriend
女朋友		girlfriend
母亲	母親	mother
妹妹		younger sister
妈妈	媽媽	Mom
我和你		you and I
姐姐		older sister
家里	家裡	at home
两个	兩個	two (of something)
哥哥		older brother
弟弟		younger brother
才一岁	才一歲	just one year old
爸爸		Dad

Review of Selected Characters and Their Radicals

The list below presents a selection of characters that have appeared so far, all of which are built with a very common radical, so common that we recommend you make these radicals objects of study. Go through the list both for review purposes and to further appreciate where the radicals appear in the characters, their shapes (especially when they change shapes) and their meanings. The list may leave the impression that some radicals are used more widely than others, and, in fact, that's quite true. However, all of these are very common.

Traditional							Simplified							
人 *rén*	你 *nǐ*	他 *tā*	們 *men*	位 *wèi*	個 *gè*	兒 *ér*	人/亻	人 *rén*	你 *nǐ*	他 *tā*	们 *men*	位 *wèi*	个 *gè*	儿 *ér*
女 *nǚ*	好 *hǎo*	姐 *jiě*	妹 *mèi*	姓 *xìng*	媽 *mā*	她 *tā*	女	女 *nǚ*	好 *hǎo*	姐 *jiě*	妹 *mèi*	姓 *xìng*	妈 *mā*	她 *tā*
嗎 *ma*	叫 *jiào*	名 *míng*	哪 *nǎ*	號 *hào*			口	吗 *ma*	叫 *jiào*	名 *míng*	哪 *nǎ*	号 *hào*		
日 *rì*	早 *zǎo*	晚 *wǎn*	星 *xīng*	時 *shí*	是 *shì*		日	日 *rì*	早 *zǎo*	晚 *wǎn*	星 *xīng*	时 *shí*	是 *shì*	
請 *qǐng*	謝 *xiè*	説 *shuō*	話 *huà*	語 *yǔ*			言/讠	请 *qǐng*	谢 *xiè*	说 *shuō*	话 *huà*	语 *yǔ*		
字 *zì*	家 *jiā*	空 *kòng*					宀	字 *zì*	家 *jiā*	空 *kòng*				
這 *zhè*	過 *guò*						辶	这 *zhè*	过 *guò*					
您 *nín*	懂 *dǒng*	想 *xiǎng*					心	您 *nín*	懂 *dǒng*	想 *xiǎng*				
地 *dì*	址 *zhǐ*						土	地 *dì*	址 *zhǐ*					
火 *huǒ*	點 *diǎn*						火/灬	火 *huǒ*	点 *diǎn*					
水 *shuǐ*	没 *méi*	法 *fǎ*					水/氵	水 *shuǐ*	没 *méi*	法 *fǎ*				

大　天 *dà*　*tiān*		大	大　天 *dà*　*tiān*
國 *guó*		口	国 *guó*
英 *yīng*		艹	英 *yīng*

父 (fù)

fù	Ancient Form	Later Form	Modern Form
father	（ancient form）	（later form）	父
fùqin			父親 / 父亲

父 (fù, 'father') in ancient times pictured a hand holding a tool or a weapon, symbolizing labor or warfare. Because working and fighting were mainly a father's responsibility (at least until more modern times), 父 came to mean 'father.' Another view of this character is as a 'hand enforcing rules with a stick.'

你很高. 你父母也都很高嗎? (高, gāo, 'tall') 　—我母親很高, 父親很矮. (矮, ǎi, 'short')	你很高. 你父母也都很高吗? (高, gāo, 'tall') 　—我母亲很高, 父亲很矮. (矮, ǎi, 'short')

父 also appears in the following words:

父子 father + son = 'father and son'	父母 father + mother = 'parents'
國父 / 国父 nation + father = 'father of the nation'	生父 birth + father = 'birth father'

爸 (bà)

bà	Ancient Form	Modern Form
dad	𦥑	爸
bàba		爸爸

爸 (bà, 'dad, pop') is a model picto-phonetic character exemplifying our strategy of learning radicals for meaning and phonetics for sound clues. 父 (fù, 'father'), on the top, is the signific component. 巴 (bā), on the bottom, is a reliable phonetic component. The upper part of 爸, 父, which you have just practiced on the preceding page, is part of 父親/父亲 (fùqin), the slightly more formal word for 'father.' 父 also serves as the first component for the word 父母 (fùmǔ, 'parents'). The more informal word for parents is 爸爸媽媽/爸爸妈妈 (bàba māma), or, more simply, 爸媽/爸妈 (bàmā), 'mom and dad.' This is, of course, reversed in the Chinese cultural order, where traditionally the male comes first.

• 我爸爸不胖 (pàng, 'fat') 也不瘦. (shòu, 'skinny')	• 我爸爸不胖 (pàng, 'fat') 也不瘦. (shòu, 'skinny')
• 我家裡只有我爸爸和 (hé, 'and') 我.	• 我家里只有我爸爸和 (hé, 'and') 我.

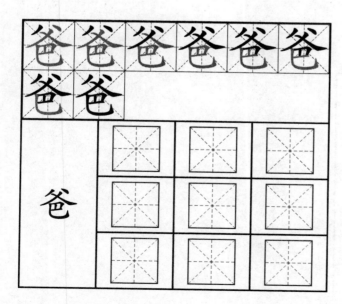

母 (mǔ)

mǔ	Ancient Form	Later Form	Modern Form
mother			母
mǔqin			母親 / 母亲

母 (*mǔ*, 'mother') pictures a kneeling woman in the ancient and later forms, but that 'picture' is perhaps less obvious in the modern version. The dots represent breasts, suggesting 'mother.'

你家裡都有甚麼人？ 　　—有媽媽, 爸爸, 繼父, 繼母. 你呢？ 　　　(繼父, *jìfù*, 'stepfather'; 繼母, *jìmǔ*, 'stepmother') 只有我和我母親.	你家里都有什么人？ 　　—有妈妈, 爸爸, 继父, 继母. 你呢？ 　　　(继父, *jìfù*, 'stepfather'; 继母, *jìmǔ*, 'stepmother') 只有我和我母亲。

母 also appears in the following words:

母愛 / 母爱 mother + love = 'maternal love'	母馬 / 母马 mother + horse = 'mare'
父母 father + mother = 'parents'	母語 / 母语 mother + language = 'mother tongue'

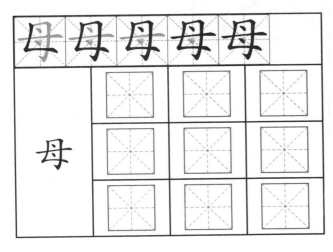

親/亲 (qīn)

qīn	Ancient Form	Later Form	Modern Traditional Form	Modern Simplified Form
parents; relatives	亲	親	親	亲
fùqin			父親	父亲

The right component of the modern traditional form of 親 (qīn, 'parents, relatives') is familiar to us. 見/见 (jiàn) of 再見/再见 (zàijiàn), you will recall, means 'to see.' Think of seeing your parents every day. Regrettably, this clue has disappeared in the simplified form.

你很高. 你父母也都很高嗎? 　　—我母親又高又瘦, 父親又矮又胖. (又 　　… 又 …, 'both … and …')	你很高. 你父母也都很高吗? 　　—我母亲又高又瘦, 父亲又矮又胖. (又 　　… 又 …, 'both … and …')

親/亲 also appears in the following words:

父母親/父母亲 father + mother + relative = 'parents'	親朋好友/亲朋好友 relatives + friends + good + friends = 'family and friends'
父親/父亲 father + parents = 'father'	親人/亲人 relative + person = 'relatives'

Modern Traditional Form	Modern Simplified Form
親 親 親 親 親 親 親 親 親 親 親 親 親 親 親 親	亲 亲 亲 亲 亲 亲 亲 亲 亲

媽/妈 (*mā*)

mā	Ancient Form	Modern Traditional Form	Modern Simplified Form
mom	孋	媽	妈
māma		媽媽	妈妈

媽/妈 (*mā*, 'mom') is a character designed to my liking. There's the radical on the left, 女 (*nǚ*, 'female'), indicating its generic meaning. And there's the phonetic 馬/马, (*mǎ*, 'horse') on the right, a quite reliable sound clue, informing us to pronounce it '*ma*.' What's more, the simplification process has left both parts intact and recognizable. This is a character to love as you would your mom.

你爸爸媽媽在哪兒？ 　　—我媽媽在英國, 爸爸在中國. 你的呢？ 爸媽兩個都在印度. (印度, *Yìndù*, 'India')	你爸爸妈妈在哪儿？ 　　—我妈妈在英国, 爸爸在中国. 你的呢？ 爸妈两个都在印度. (印度, *Yìndù*, 'India')

Modern Traditional Form	Modern Simplified Form
媽 媽 媽 媽 媽 媽 媽 媽 媽 媽 媽 媽 媽	妈 妈 妈 妈 妈 妈
媽	妈

姐 (jiě)

jiě	Ancient Form	Modern Form
elder sister	姐	姐
jiějie		姐姐

姐 (*jiě*) is a typical radical-plus-phonetic character. 女 (*nǔ*, 'woman'), on the left, provides the class of meaning, while 且 (*qiě*), on the right, is the phonetic component. You might argue that *qiě* is not *jiě* and you'd be right. But, just as radicals suggest only a class of meaning, so phonetics give, in most cases, a sound class. It's rare that either gives a 100 percent direct route to meaning or pronunciation, but they will help you. Chinese people, when learning and reading Chinese, use such clues constantly.

• 我有一個哥哥, 兩個弟弟, 三個姐姐. • 我沒有哥哥姐姐, 只有兩個弟弟. • 我姐姐和她丈夫都在英國. (丈夫, *zhàngfu*, 'husband')	• 我有一个哥哥, 两个弟弟, 三个姐姐. • 我没有哥哥姐姐, 只有两个弟弟. • 我姐姐和她丈夫都在英国. (丈夫, *zhàngfu*, 'husband')

姐 also appears in the following words:

姐妹 elder sister + younger sister = 'sibling; sisters'	小姐 little + sister = 'Miss' (Li, Jones, etc.)
空姐 air (*kōng*) + sister = 'airline stewardess'	大姐 old(er) + sister = 'older sister'

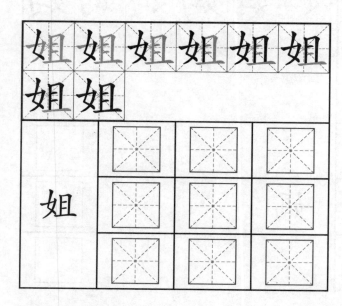

妹 (*mèi*)

mèi	Ancient Form	Later Form	Modern Form
younger sister	𡥟	𣚼	妹
mèimei			妹妹

妹 (*mèi*, 'younger sister'). By now the radical of this character should be familiar to you. You've seen it in 好 (*hǎo*), 姓 (*xìng*), 媽/妈 (*mā*), and also 姐 (*jiě*). 妹 combines nicely with 姐 to form 姐妹 (*jiěmèi*, 'sisters'), the 'companion' word to 兄弟 (*xiōngdì*, 'brothers'). We also have 兄弟姐妹 (*xiōngdì jiěmèi*), which provides us with 'siblings.' By the way, 未 (*wei*) on the right is the phonetic.

我家裡人很多. 有兄弟也有姐妹. 兩個哥哥, 三個弟弟, 四個妹妹, 一個姐姐.   —真多! (真, *zhēn*, 'really')

我家里人很多。有兄弟也有姐妹。两个哥哥, 三个弟弟, 四个妹妹, 一个姐姐.   —真多! (真, *zhēn*, 'really')

妹 妹 妹 妹 妹 妹
妹 妹

妹

兄 (*xiōng*)

xiōng	Ancient Form	Later Form	Modern Form
elder brother	𝍐	兄	兄
xiōngdì			兄弟

兄 (*xiōng*, 'elder brother') is an interesting character with 口 (*kǒu*, 'mouth') on top and a slightly altered 人 (*rén*, 'person') on the bottom. Throughout Chinese history, age has implied authority. So elder brother trumps younger brother. 'Mouth' on top means elder brother is in 'charge' of younger siblings, male or female. Elder brother does the 'talking,' except, of course, when others older than he are involved.

你有兄弟姐妹嗎？ 　—我沒有兄弟，可是有三個姐妹，都很小， 　　你呢？(可是, *kěshì*, 'but') 沒有兄弟姐妹. 我是獨生子. (獨生子, 　　*dúshēngzǐ*, 'only child')	你有兄弟姐妹吗？ 　—我没有兄弟，可是有三个姐妹，都很小， 　　你呢？(可是, *kěshì*, 'but') 没有兄弟姐妹. 我是独生子. (独生子, 　　*dúshēngzǐ*, 'only child')

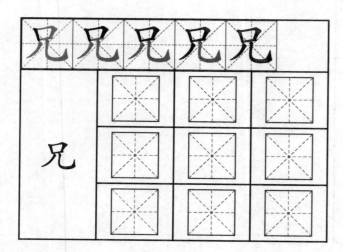

哥 (gē)

gē	Ancient Form	Modern Form
(older) brother	哥	哥
gēge		哥哥

哥 (*gē*, [older] 'brother') is an interesting 'top-bottom' character. The top is repeated by the bottom. And both the top and the bottom are characters in themselves, and common ones at that. Both are forms of 可 (*kě*) and part of two very useful words: 可是 (*kěshì*, 'but; however'), and 可以 (*kěyi*, 'can, may'). Pile 可 upon 可 and you get 哥.

你有哥哥姐姐嗎? 　—有, 有, 有. 有三個哥哥, 四個姐姐. 哎喲 (*āiyō*, 'wow'), 你家裡人真多!	你有哥哥姐姐吗? 　—有, 有, 有。有三个哥哥, 四个姐姐. 哎哟 (*āiyō*, 'wow'), 你家里人真多!

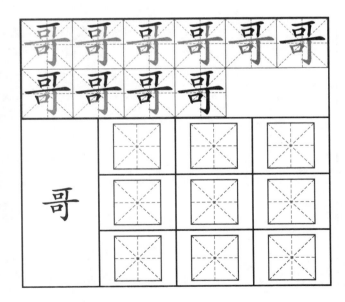

弟 (*dì*)

dì	Ancient Form	Later Form	Modern Form
(younger) brother	ϸ	弟	弟
dìdi			弟弟

弟 (*dì*, 'younger brother') suggests a spindle with thread or string wrapped 'orderly' around it. Thus its association with 'order' or 'sequence' and, therefore, 'birth sequence.' If you are the elder brother, 哥哥 (*gēge*), your 弟弟 (*dìdi*) follows you in birth sequence.

你弟弟幾歲？ 　　—弟弟很小. 才三歲。	你弟弟几岁？ 　　—弟弟很小. 才三岁.

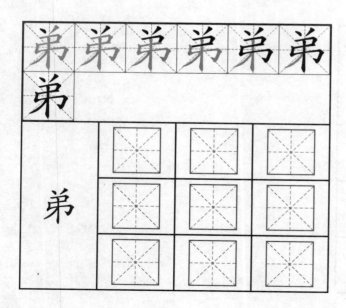

男 (*nán*)

nán	Ancient Form	Later Form	Modern Form
man; male	𭆊	𤰚	男
nán péngyou			男朋友

男 (*nán*, 'male, man') is a top-bottom character composed of 田 (*tián*, 'field') (slightly flattened) with 力 (*lì*, 'strength') on the bottom. Although things are rapidly changing in China, as elsewhere, in traditional China it was the man who was associated with labor in the fields. 男 appears in many compound words relating to 'man; male.'

Here are some useful words with 男 and some opposites with 女 (*nǚ*).

男的 *nánde* male	男人 *nánrén* man	男朋友 *nán péngyou* boyfriend	男孩子 *nán háizi* young boy	男老師/师 *nán lǎoshī* male teacher	男生 *nánshēng* male student; teenager (boy)
女的 *nǚde* female	女人 *nǚrén* woman	女朋友 *nǚ péngyou* girlfriend	女孩子 *nǚ háizi* young girl	女老師/师 *nǚ lǎoshī* female teacher	女生 *nǚshēng* female student; teenager (girl)

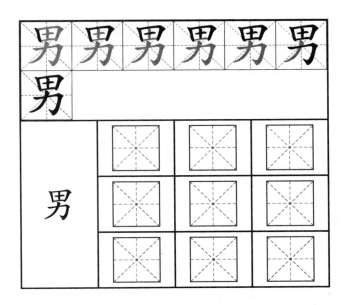

女 (nǚ)

nǚ	Ancient Form	Later Form	Modern Form
woman			女
nǚ péngyou			女朋友

The character 女 (*nǚ*) is a pictographic character, in the ancient form a drawing of a kneeling woman. 女 is also a common radical providing a semantic link to many characters having to deal with various aspects of womanhood. Here are a few examples, some you already know and some you will come to know in your future with Chinese. Note the position of the radical as well. Find the one that seems to have no relation at all to the meaning 'woman.' How many do you recognize? How many can you define?

她 (她們 / 们)	女孩
好 (好看)	女孩子
姓 (姓王)	女人
姐 (姐姐)	女生
妹 (妹妹)	女子
安 (天安門 / 天安门)	女士
如 (如果)	男女
女兒 / 女儿	女工
子女	女王
兒女 / 儿女	妈妈

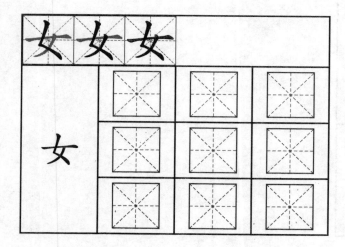

兩/两 (*liǎng*)

liǎng	Ancient Form	Modern Traditional Form	Modern Simplified Form
two; a couple of	兩	兩	两
liǎng ge		兩個	两个

兩/两 (*liǎng*, 'two; a couple of') shows us, in all its forms, a rather clear picture of a 'two-wheeled horse-drawn vehicle.' The horizontal line on the top is the vehicle, and the bottom part is somewhat like the yoke, a crossbar with two U-shaped pieces that encircle the necks of a pair of horses working together. The simplified form preserves the image. In fact, the simplified form seems to have two persons (人, *rén*) within it.

兩個名字	两个名字
兩位老師	两位老师
兩點半	两点半
兩個家	两个家
兩個弟弟	两个弟弟
兩個晚上	两个晚上
兩天	两天

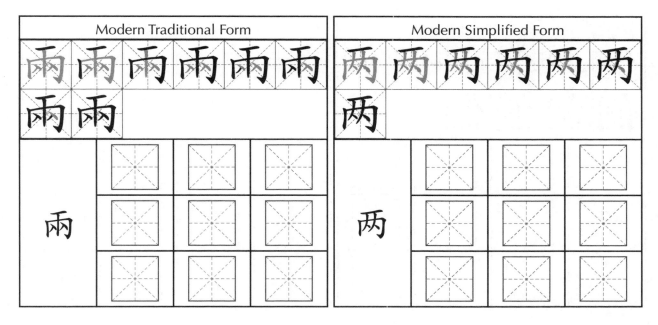

個/个 (gè)

gè	Modern Traditional Form	Modern Simplified Form
a; one (*general measure word*)	個	个
yí gè	一個	一个

個/个 (*gè*) offers a nice memory aid, at least in the simplified character. The modern simplified form is formed with 人 (*rén*, 'person')—a radical you've run into several times—and a "standing" 一 (*yī*, 'one,' the vertical stroke). Let's consider that stroke 'a; one.' The traditional character combines 亻('a standing man') with 固 (*gù*), the phonetic component, on the right.

一個/一个　兩個/两个　哪個/哪个?　那個/那个　這個/这个　幾個/几个?

你家有幾個人? 　—我家有六個人. 爸爸媽媽, 兩個妹妹, 　一個弟弟. 還有我.	你家有几个人? 　—我家有六个人. 爸爸妈妈, 两个妹妹, 　一个弟弟, 还有我.

Modern Traditional Form	Modern Simplified Form
個個個個個個 個個個個	个个个

和 (hé)

hé	Ancient Form	Modern Form
and; with	咊	和
Wǒ hé nǐ qù.		我和你去.

和 (hé) has two obvious parts. On the left there is 'grain,' implying agriculture. On the right is a 'mouth,' signifying something spoken. Both 'grain' and 'mouth' involve a plural effort: conversation must be a two-way endeavor, while farming, of course, involves a group or communal effort, suggesting 'with; and.'

• 我家裡只有我和我父母.	• 我家里只有我和我父母.
• 我姐姐和我弟弟都在中國.	• 我姐姐和我弟弟都在中国.
• 我和你去, 行不行?	• 我和你去, 行不行?
• 美國和中國都很大, 都是大國.	• 美国和中国都很大, 都是大国.

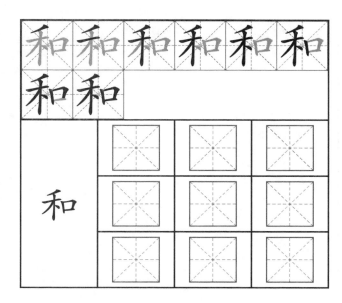

才 (*cái*)

cái	Ancient Form	Later Form	Modern Form
just; only	↓	才	才
cái yí suì			才一歲／才一岁

才 (*cái*, 'only') is a picture of a sprouting plant, a plant only just now coming forth from the ground. It is so tiny, just a seedling. Distinguish 才 and 只 (*zhǐ*), in meaning, both seen in this unit, both meaning 'only.' 才 is directly followed by a number, while 只 is often seen preceeding the verb 有 (*yǒu*, 'have; there is'), rendering the meanings 'only,' 'only have,' or 'there is only.'

• 我孩子才一歲. My child is only one year old.	• 我孩子才一岁. My child is only one year old.
• 我家裡只有我和我父母, 没有兄弟姐妹. There are only me and my parents in my family, no brothers or sisters.	• 我家里只有我和我父母, 没有兄弟姐妹. There are only me and my parents in my family, no brothers or sisters.
• 你妹妹弟弟幾歲了? —妹妹十歲了, 弟弟才一歲.	• 你妹妹弟弟几岁了? —妹妹十岁了, 弟弟才一岁.
• 你有哥哥姐姐嗎? —没有. 我没有兄弟姐妹.	• 你有哥哥姐姐吗? —没有. 我没有兄弟姐妹.

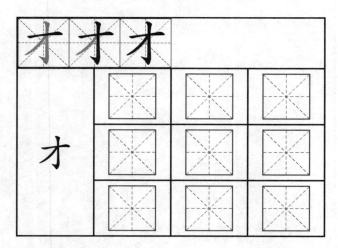

lǐ	Ancient Form	Modern Traditional Form	Modern Simplified Form
in; inside	里	裡	里
jiālǐ		家裡	家里

In ancient times, both 里 and 裡 existed side by side. 里, then and now, was a distance of measure, like a mile. 裡 (also written as 裏) meant 'lining (of clothing)' and therefore was used to provide the meaning 'inside.' 裡 and 裏 have 里 as the phonetic component, although you must look carefully at 裏 to find the 里. The radical/meaning clue in both traditional forms is 衤 (full form 衣, 'clothing'). The Chinese faced many problems 'designing' their characters but never ran out of solutions. To recap, if you learn the modern traditional characters, you will encounter three forms: 裡 and 里 and sometimes 裏. If you concentrate on simplified characters, you will only encounter 里.

你家裡都有甚麼人？ 　　—我家裡人很多．爸爸，媽媽，一個哥哥， 　　兩個弟弟，三個姐姐和四個妹妹。 真不少．(真, *zhēn*, 'truly, really')	你家里都有什么人？ 　　—我家里人很多．爸爸，妈妈，一个哥哥， 　　两个弟弟，三个姐姐和四个妹妹． 真不少．(真, *zhēn*, 'truly, really')

Modern Traditional Form	Modern Simplified Form
裡 裡 裡 裡 裡 裡 裡 裡 裡 裡 裡 裡 裡	里 里 里 里 里 里 里

Unit 6

The sentences below are inspired by the contents of Unit 6 and contain most of the new characters required for writing as well as others. Read and reread until fluent, covering the English as you read. Then cover the English and try to reproduce the Chinese equivalents. Do this until fluent.

她念四年级. 她念四年級.	She's in the fourth grade.
学中文很有意思. 學中文很有意思.	Studying Chinese is very interesting.
我很想赚点儿钱. 我很想賺點兒錢.	I want to earn some money.
谁知道将来的事情? 誰知道將來的事情?	Who knows about future events?
我不知道她姓什么. 我不知道她姓甚麼.	I don't know what her last name is.
她也会做饭. 她也會做飯.	She can cook too.
这个或者那个都行. 這個或者那個都行.	Either this or that will do.
因为你去, 所以我也要去. 因為你去, 所以我也要去.	Since you're going, I want to go too.
你明天想做什么? 你明天想做甚麼?	What do you want to do tomorrow?
我不知道她将来要当什么. 我不知道她將來要當甚麼.	I don't know what she wants to be in the future.

It All Started with Oracle Bones

Just where did Chinese characters come from? For an answer to how the most ancient Chinese characters were discovered, we need to go back to the beginning of the twentieth century, a time of trouble for China, a nation then suffering with drought, famine, disease, weak imperial government, and war with foreign powers. The peasants around the village of Xiao Tun (小吞) in northern Hunan (湖南) province, like millions of others, tilled their soil but often turned up a curious harvest: bits of bone thought by the peasants to have been shed by ancient dragons. Long-held superstition had convinced them that these bone-treasures held magic powers. Some were further convinced of such powers by the strange symbols, scratches really, that they found incised on them. In exchange for a few copper coins, apothecaries in nearby Peking (Beijing) bought the bones up eagerly, grinding them into a magic medicinal powder for a broth said to cure most anything that ailed anyone. Eventually, by one of those strange chances that history is full of, some of these bones fell into the hands of Chinese scholars who determined that those odd inscriptions actually held secrets of China's far-off past. After years of study, Chinese and Western scholars alike concluded that the objects found in the farmlands of Xiao Tun were not 'dragon bones' but the bones of cattle and tortoises used in ancient times to divine the will of heaven and the minds of gods. The inscriptions incised on these bones, later called 'oracle bones' (jiǎgǔ, 甲骨), represent the earliest form of Chinese writing but not, as one would suspect, a primitive form of language. Rather, they reveal a writing system in which every important principle in the formation of Chinese characters was already in use, and this system was used approximately 1,500 years before the birth of Christ. The information revealed on these thousands of specimens depicts a civilization in China that had already reached a high level of sophistication.

How were the oracle bones used? The Chinese priest, the oracle, forecasted the future in an unusual way, with unusual materials. When asked by his king what the future held, he used the flat bones of cattle or tortoises, placed them in a fire, and waited for cracks to appear in the bones. The oracle interpreted the cracks to answer the king's query. The king was interested in many things, everything from how the weather would be for hunting tomorrow to how his army would perform in battle. And now the important part for us: Chinese characters were used to inscribe a question onto the bone fragment—not only the question, but the priest-oracle's answer, and not only that, but the date of the question and sometimes even whether the prediction eventually proved true or false. All of this is great information for historians, archeologists, and, of course, those concerned with the development of Chinese written language. Thousands of oracle bones have been unearthed and read with a fair degree of accuracy, and from them we've learned a lot about China and the Chinese written language.

What does an oracle bone look like? Just Google "oracle bones" and you will find a pile of information.

也 (yě)

yě	Ancient Form	Modern Form
also; too; as well	ⵂ	也
Wǒ yě hěn hǎo.		我也很好.

也 (*yě*) in ancient times was a pictograph of a washbasin, perhaps discernible from the ancient form. Well, it's a very long way from 'washbasin' to its modern meaning of 'also.' My guess is that 也 is another example of a 'loan character.' The ancient Chinese must have regarded their inventory of characters as a sort of 'bank' from which one might borrow existing characters to perform new meanings, without changing their shape. So 'washbasin' became 'also.' For us it's important to distinguish 也 from the following lookalikes. Do you recall them? 他 她 地 Here's something interesting: give 也 a bath by adding the water radical to the left, and you get the Chinese character for 'pool,' 池 (*chí*).

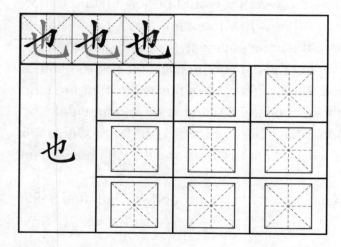

tā	Ancient Form	Modern Form
she; her	姕	她
Tā yǒu jiěmèi ma?		她有姐妹吗?

More and more you're beginning to come across components that you have seen before. Here are two familiar ones bound together in a new meaning. Here, in 她 *(tā)*, 女 *(nǚ,* 'female') on the left is the radical, providing a generic range of meaning, while 也, on the right, is unsatisfying as a phonetic but is, at least, a familiar component. 她 is a character of recent common usage. For many years in Chinese texts, 他 *(tā)* served both as 'he; him' as well as 'she; her.' Of course, in the spoken language, 他 and 她 are pronounced identically, so it mattered not at all in speech. It is only in the modern written language that 'he' and 'she' are distinguished by different characters.

Here's a review of characters bearing the 女 radical.

好　姐　妹　姓　妈/媽　她

Do you recognize all of them? Can you use each in a sentence or phrase?

她 她 她 她 她 她

她

還/还 (hái)

hái	Ancient Form	Modern Traditional Form	Modern Simplified Form
still; yet; or	還	還	还
háishì		還是	还是

We all remember 不 (*bù*, 'no'), but we may not remember the ancient meaning of *bù*: 'bird rising to heaven.' Well, that bird is <u>still</u> rising in 还 (*hái*), and the meaning is aided further by the addition of 辶, the radical for 'road; walk; go,' which we have seen before in *zhè* 這/这 and *guò* 過/过 and *dào* 道 of 知道 (*zhīdào*, 'to know'). Some of you may have learned the character 遠/远 (*yuǎn*, 'far'), which also employs 辶. 睘 (*huán*), on the right, is the phonetic component, but how that leads us to *hái* is beyond me. Let's chalk it up to language change over the centuries. By the way, remember to keep *háishì* and *huòzhě* 或者 distinct. Both can mean 'or.' See textbook page 161.

你最近怎麼樣?—還可以.	你最近怎么样?—还可以
他來了嗎?—還沒來呢.	他来了吗?—还没来呢.
這個好還是那個好?—都好.	这个好还是那个好?—都好.

Modern Traditional Form	Modern Simplified Form
還	还

Copyright © 2012 by Yale University and China International Publishing Group

想 (*xiǎng*)

xiǎng	Ancient Form	Modern Form
want to; would like to; think (one might)	想	想
Wǒ hěn xiǎng qù.		我很想去.

想 (*xiǎng*) is another combination character, a marriage of radical and phonetic. Can you find the relevant radical? (There are three radicals in this character.) It's the bottom element, of course, 心 (*xīn*), meaning 'heart/mind,' and thus it is the link to 'wanting to,' 'thinking one might,' etc. You've seen the 心 radical before in 懂 and 您. Notice how it changes shape when it forms part of a component character, like 懂. 相, at the top, is the phonetic; it is pronounced *xiāng*, but in the first tone. Memory aid? 'Wanting to; desiring to; planning to' all begin in the 'heart.' Incidentally, the other two radicals in 想 are 'tree' 木 and 'eye' 目.

你將來想賺錢還是想幫別人? —我又想賺錢又想幫別人.	你将来想赚钱还是想帮别人? —我又想赚钱又想帮别人.
想家 think + home = 'homesick'	想到 think + to; reach = 'think of; call to mind'
想法 think + way; method = 'idea'	想一想 think + one + think = 'think it over'

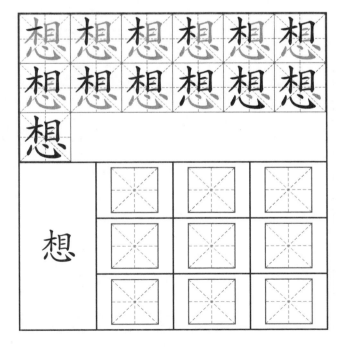

yào	Ancient Form	Later Form	Modern Form
want to; will, going to; important			要
Wǒ bú yào chūqù.			我不要出去.

要 (*yào*) is tough to analyze. Originally a picture of 'hands girdling a waist,' and therefore 'waist,' 要 was later borrowed to express the meaning of 'middle; important.' From 'important,' 要 got its extended meaning of 'to demand; want.' Modern Chinese now uses the character 腰 (*yāo*) for 'waist,' adding the radical 月 ('body') to 要. I can't figure out why the 女 (*nǚ*, 'woman') character is at the bottom. What do you think?

要人 important + person = 'very important person, a VIP'	要事 important + thing; matter = 'important matter'
想要 would like to + want = 'want, feel like'	要是 will; might + be = 'if'

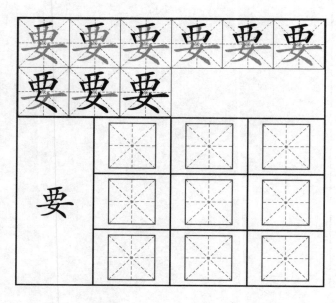

將/将 (*jiāng*)

jiāng	Ancient Form	Modern Traditional Form	Modern Simplified Form
(forms a compound word with *lái* 來/来)	將	將	将
jiānglái		將來	将来

將/将 is another typical radical-plus-phonetic character, but it was always tough to come up with a memory aid for it. But then I learned the character for 'soy sauce,' which is 醬 (*jiàng*), a character with 將/将 *jiāng* on top and a version of 酒 (*jiǔ*, 'wine') on the bottom. I linked these two for recognition, keeping their meanings separate, of course. Remember that 將/将 combines with 來/来 *lái*, producing 將來/将来 (*jiānglái*, 'in the future'). Is there soy sauce in your future? I'll bet there is! Note: 'soy sauce' in Chinese is 醬油 (*jiàngyóu*).

你將來想當甚麼？ 　—我將來想當老師或者作家. (作家, *zuòjiā*, 'writer')	你将来想当什么？ 　—我将来想当老师或者作家. (作家, *zuòjiā*, 'writer')

Modern Traditional Form	Modern Simplified Form
將 將 將 將 將 將 將 將 將 將 將　　將	将 将 将 将 将 将 将 将 将　　将

lái	Ancient Form	Later Form	Modern Traditional Form	Modern Simplified Form
come			來	来
jiānglái			將來	将来

來/来 (*lái*) is the character that many analysts point to as most exemplifying the phonetic loan process. Remember that phonetic loan characters are those already existing characters borrowed for use because of phonetic similiarites to represent new meanings. The ancient meaning of 來/来 was 'ears of wheat hanging from the wheat plant.' Once the ears are seen, the harvest is coming. Maybe that's why the ancients used (future) 'ears of wheat' to represent 'come.' The meaning of 'come' makes 來/来 a great candidate for pairing with *jiāng* 將/将 in the compound 將來/将来 (*jiānglái*)—the 'coming time,' that is, the 'future.'

你知道你將來要當甚麽？ 　—不知道. 誰知道將來的事？	你知道你將來要当什么？ 　—不知道. 谁知道將来的事？

Modern Traditional Form

Modern Simplified Form

賺/赚 (*zhuàn*)

zhuàn	Ancient Form	Modern Traditional Form	Modern Simplified Form
to earn	賺	賺	赚
zhuàn qián		賺錢	赚钱

賺/赚 (*zhuàn*, 'to earn'), is another typical radical-plus-phonetic character. The radical here is 貝 (*bèi*), new to us, a pictograph of a cowrie shell. Now shells were used in ancient times for money, so hereafter when you see 貝 in other characters, think 'money,' or money-related activities, or anything of value. The right component is the phonetic 兼 (*jiān*), which is not a very reliable sound clue, however. You perhaps have already learned, or will soon, two very useful characters with the 貝 radical. Here they are: 買/买 (*mǎi*, 'to buy, purchase'). Notice the considerable simplification: 賣/卖 (*mài*, 'to sell'). Again, notice that the simplification process has radically changed both of these characters and, in fact, eliminated the valuable 貝 component, resulting in two very similar simplified forms, often confused by beginning students.

Modern Traditional Form	Modern Simplified Form

賺	賺	賺	賺	賺	賺
賺	賺	賺	賺	賺	賺
賺	賺	賺	賺	賺	

赚	赚	赚	赚	赚	赚
赚	赚	赚	赚	赚	赚
赚	赚				

賺

赚

錢/钱 (*qián*)

qián	Ancient Form	Modern Traditional Form	Modern Simplified Form
money	錢	錢	钱
zhuàn qián		賺錢	赚钱

錢/钱 (*qián*) is another typical radical-plus-phonetic or picto-phonetic character. In ancient time, currency, in the absence of paper, was made of metal, so on the left is the radical whose meaning relates to 'metal,' 金 (*jīn*) (which also means 'gold,' by the way). Some regard the 'dots' in the lower part of the radical as 'nuggets,' which have disappeared in the simplified radical, thereby saving three strokes of the pen.

有人说, 錢多好. 我说錢夠就好. (夠/够, *gòu*, 'enough; sufficient')	有人说, 钱多好. 我说钱够就好. (夠/够, *gòu*, 'enough; sufficient')
有錢/有钱 have + money = 'be rich, wealthy'	没錢/没钱 be without + money = 'be poor; be broke'

Modern Traditional Form	Modern Simplified Form
錢 錢 錢 錢 錢 錢 錢 錢 錢 錢 錢 錢 錢 錢 錢 錢	钱 钱 钱 钱 钱 钱 钱 钱 钱 钱
錢	钱

因 (*yīn*)

yīn	Ancient Form	Later Form	Modern Form
because; since	大	因	因
yīnwèi			因為 / 因为

Look carefully inside 因 (*yīn*) and you'll see an old friend. It's 大 (*dà*, 'large, big'). Remember that 大 is a pictograph of a person with arms extended, indicating 'big.' Let's take 因 as a person lying on a mat for no reason at all, just because he wants to. Keep in mind that 因 為 / 因为 (*yīnwèi*) often appears with two related words: 為甚麼 / 为什么 (*wèishénme*, 'why') and 所以 (*suǒyǐ*, 'therefore').

你為甚麼不去？ 　　—因為他不要去, 所以我也不去.	你为什么不去？ 　　—因为他不要去, 所以我也不去.

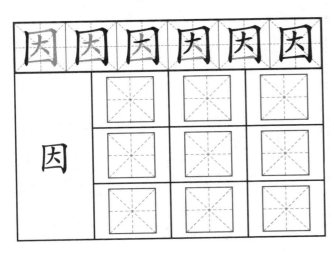

為/为 (wèi)

wèi	Ancient Form	Later Form	Modern Traditional Form	Modern Simplified Form
for	𩕃	𧰧	為	为
yīnwèi			因為	因为
wèishénme			為甚麼	为什么

What was the meaning of the original pictograph for 為/为? Some say 為 (wèi) pictured a female monkey, while others maintain the ancient form was a 'person's hand leading an elephant, training the beast to work.' The later form above seems to resemble the latter explanation to me, but neither is much help. Why a monkey? Why an elephant? 爲/為/为 is probably a loan character. Let's leave it at that unless you have a better idea. Note that there are two traditional forms: 為 and 爲. You'll see both forms in traditional character texts.

你為甚麼要當醫生?(yīsheng, 'doctor') 因為我父母要我當醫生.	你为什么要当医生?(yīsheng, 'doctor') 因为我父母要我当医生.

Modern Traditional Form	Modern Simplified Form
為 為 為 為 為 為 為 為 為	为 为 为 为
為	为

bāng	Ancient Form	Modern Traditional Form	Modern Simplified Form
help; assist	幫	幫	帮
bāng biérén		幫別人	帮別人

幫/帮 is a perhaps the most complicated character we've seen so far. Seventeen strokes and at least four components! No wonder 幫 was a prime candidate for simplification, turning into 帮, which still has three components. The component that carried over in the process is 巾 *jīn*, which is a picture of a 'hanging towel; cloth; handkerchief'—all things that are useful when helping or being helped. By the way, the simplified form uses *bāng* 邦 as the phonetic, which is part of the word meaning 'utopia,' *wūtuōbāng*—a place where no one needs help.

幫忙/帮忙 help + busy = 'help'	幫助/帮助 help + aid = 'help; aid'

Modern Traditional Form	Modern Simplified Form

知 (*zhī*)

zhī	Ancient Form	Later Form	Modern Form
know	智	知	知
zhīdào			知道

知 (*zhī*) means 'to know.' It is composed of 'arrow' 矢 (*shǐ*) and the by now familiar 口 (*kǒu*, 'mouth'). Some people remember this character with this memory aid: if one knows something, one will be able to put it into speech as quickly as an arrow flying forth from a bow. The ancient form pictures a person shooting a bow and arrow, so think 'arrow-like intelligence' and you get 'in the know.' Caution: *zhīdao* (affirmative) is pronounced with a neutral tone on *dao*; however, *bù zhīdào* (negative) is usually pronounced with the fourth tone on *dao*. Another caution: distinguish *zhīdào* ('to know, be aware' [of something]) from 認識/认识 (*rènshi*, 'to know/recognize' [someone]). 很高興認識你! / 很高兴认识你! *Hěn gāoxìng rènshi nǐ.*

• 我不知道他姓甚麼.	• 我不知道他姓什么.
• 你知道那件事嗎?	• 你知道那件事吗?

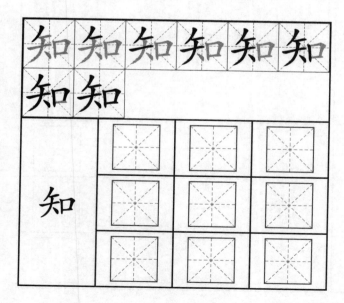

道 *(dào)*

dào	Ancient Form	Modern Form
road; way; path	邎	道
zhīdào		知道

道 (*dào*) means 'path; road,' the path to 'knowledge.' The character combines 辶, the radical for 'go,' with 首, 'head' (see the 'hair' on top). To 'know' is to make some effort (go) with your 'head.' When you get your head going, you're in the 'know,' you *zhīdao*! (知道).

我不知道我將來要當甚麼.	我不知道我将来要当什么.
知道 know + the way = 'know'	小道 small + way, road = 'a side road; byway'

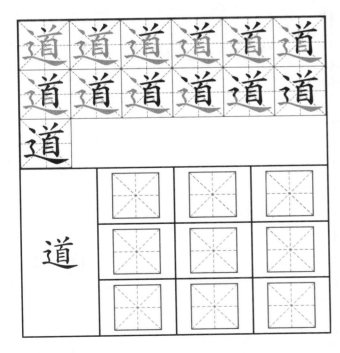

當/当 (dāng)

dāng	Ancient Form	Modern Traditional Form	Modern Simplified Form
work as; serve as	當	當	当
dāng lǎoshī		當老師	当老师

當/当 (*dāng*), in the early form and modern traditional form, has 田 ('a piece of cultivated land') at the bottom. Well, 'cultivated land,' in the East or West—anywhere, for that matter—spells 'work,' and 當/当 means 'to work as.' 當/当 reminds me of the character 男 (*nán*), which also has the component 田. Unfortunately, 田 disappears in the simplified equivalent. The simplification process, as you have noticed, has certainly resulted in a reduction in strokes, making characters easier to write, but has, in many cases, removed memory clues that may have proven useful to learners.

Can you understand these seven career choices?

當醫生	當工人	當司機	當老師	當演員	當經理	當歌星
当医生	当工人	当司机	当老师	当演员	当经理	当歌星

Modern Traditional Form	Modern Simplified Form
當 當 當 當 當 當 當 當 當 當 當 當 當	当 当 当 当 当 当
當	当

zuò	Ancient Form	Modern Form
do; make; engage in	做	做
zuò fàn		做飯 / 做饭

做 (*zuò*) means 'to do; to make,' or, by extension, with the appropriate noun appended, 'to engage in some activity,' like manual work, carpentry, writing a poem, or even going to church. As you've seen before in many characters, the radical is the left part, the 'standing man,' 亻, because it's a person doing the action. The right component, 故 (*gù*), means 'cause,' so 'cause to happen,' that is, 'do.' Here are some examples showing how wide ranging 做 is; this can also serve as a vocabulary review, although one or two might be new to you. Work out the meanings with your classmates.

• 做愛 / 做爱 (*zuò ài*) • 做事 (*zuò shì*) • 做買賣 / 做买卖 (*zuò mǎimài*)	• 做早飯 / 做中飯 / 做晚飯 做早饭 / 做中饭 / 做晚饭 (*zuò zǎofàn* / *zuò zhōngfàn* / *zuò wǎnfàn*)

做 做 做 做 做 做
做 做 做 做 做

做

别 (bié)

bié	Ancient Form	Modern Forms
other; another; don't	𢧀	别 別
biérén		别人

别 (*bié*, 'others') has a common radical on the right side. The radical is 刀/刂 (*dāo*, 'knife'), so it's associated with cutting apart, making separate, creating others. Remember 刀? You saw 刀 in its full form in 'a fraction of an hour; a minute'—namely, 分 (*fēn*). Note above that two slightly different forms of *bié* are seen in modern texts. We prefer 别. Keep in mind that just as English has different fonts, so does Chinese.

别人 other + person = 'other people'	别的 other + *de* = 'other; another'
分别 divide + cut apart = 'to separate'	别忘了 don't + forget + *le* = 'Don't forget.'

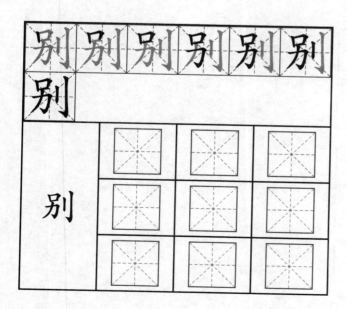

或 (*huò*)

huò	Ancient Form	Later Form	Modern Form
or; perhaps	或	或	或
huòzhě			或者

或 (*huò*) should remind you of another character, learned some time ago. Recall the traditional character 國 (*guó*) and notice that 'inside' of 國 is 或. Asssociate one with the other (they even rhyme!). As you learn one, try to link it with the other. Interestingly enough, the original meaning of 或 was 'country.' The language, in need of a word to represent 'or,' borrowed 或 in the 'phonetic loan' process. Keep in mind that 或者 ('or') is used in statements, while 還是/还是 (*háishì*), which also means 'or,' is used in questions.

• 我父母说, 我上大學或者去工作都可以. • 我將來不想當醫生或者護士. • 這個好還是那個好?
• 我父母说, 我上大学或者去工作都可以. • 我将来不想当医生或者护士. • 这个好还是那个好?

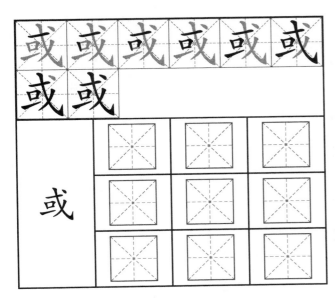

者 (zhě)

zhě	Ancient Form	Later Form	Modern Form
(component of *huòzhě*, 'or')	者 (ancient glyph)	者 (later glyph)	者
huòzhě			或者

Anayzing the structure and meaning of 者 (*zhě*) is a bit tough. The ancient form is no help to me, but it does look interesting. I've got no memory aid for 者. It's just one of those that simply must be memorized. Notice 日 (*rì*, 'sun') in the southeast corner. Most relevant for us in this unit is the compound 或者 (*huòzhě*, 'or'). Relevant for your future in Chinese is this character's role as a suffix to verbs. Put a limited set of verbs in front of 者 and its meaning becomes 'one who (does the verb).' Example: 學者/学者 (*xuézhě*), 'one who studies'; therefore, a 'scholar.' Be careful to distinguish 者 from its structural look-alike 都 (*dōu* 'all'). Also: distinguish 或者 from its meaning look-alike 還是/还是 (*háishi*).

• 你去或者我去, 都可以.   • 上大學或者去工作都行.
• 你去或者我去, 都可以.   • 上大学或者去工作都行.

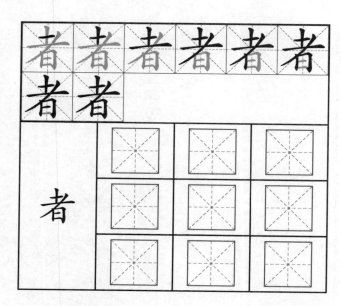

念 (niàn)

niàn	Ancient Form	Later Form	Modern Form
read; study; attend school	𠙵	念	念
niàn sān niánjí			念三年級 / 念三年级

By now, the radical in 念 (*niàn*) should be familiar to you. Its connection to meaning should also be evident. Recall 您, 懂, and 想 for other examples of characters whose meaning is linked, directly or indirectly, to the radical 心 (*xīn*, 'heart, mind') in 念. The relevant meaning for 念 that interests us is 'read; study; attend school,' or, by extension, 'to attend school in a certain grade.' Notice the top part as well. The ancient form has 口 ('mouth') on the top. The modern form has 今. Do you recall 今, as in 今天?

• 他念過中學, 没上過大學. • 我哥哥念八年級, 弟弟上二年級. • 我不工作, 我念書. (*niànshū*, 'attend school')	• 他念过中学, 没上过大学. • 我哥哥念八年级, 弟弟上二年级. • 我不工作, 我念书. (*niànshū*, 'attend school')

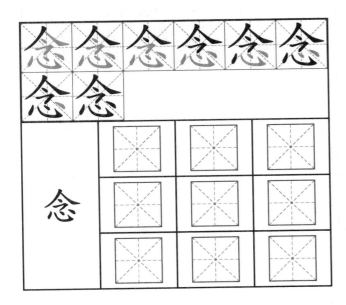

級/级 (jí)

jí	Ancient Form	Modern Traditional Form	Modern Simplified Form
a grade; a class at school	繇	級	级
sān niánjí		三年級	三年级

級/级 (*jí*) is a typical, side-by-side, double-component, radical-plus-phonetic character. 糸 / 纟 (*sī*), on the left, is the meaning component, 'thread' or 'silk,' and by extension, the quality of silk thread, the grade of silk, thus enabling us with a bit of imagining to reach the compound 年級/年级 (*niánjí*, 'year in school; grade'). 及 (*jí*), on the right, is the very reliable phonetic component, which, by the way, means 'reach; attain' a certain 'level' or 'grade.' So both sides support one another in meaning while at the same time providing the radical and the phonetic.

我大妹妹上初中七年級, 小妹妹上三年級.	我大妹妹上初中七年级, 小妹妹上三年级.
上級 / 上级 above, up + level = 'superior'	下級 / 下级 below + level = 'subordinate'
年級 / 年级 year + level = 'grade'	幾年級 / 几年级 = 'what grade in school?'

Modern Traditional Form	Modern Simplified Form
級 級 級 級 級 級 級 級 級 級	级 级 级 级 级
級	级

意 (yì)

yì	Ancient Form	Modern Form
meaning; a thought; an idea	𢒈	意
yǒu yìsi		有意思

意 (yì) has two components, 音 (yīn, 'speech; sound') and, below it, 心 (xīn, 'heart'). Listen carefully to the 'sounds' of your 'heart/mind' and you'll surely come up with an 'idea' that will be 'interesting'—that is, 有意思, yǒu yìsi.

我要有一個有意思的工作.	我要有一个有意思的工作.
中文真有意思, 我很想學.	中文真有意思, 我很想学.
意见 thought + see = 'view, opinion'	意外的事 thought + outside + de + affair = 'something unexpected/unforeseen'
有意思 have meaning + think = 'interesting'	没意思 without + idea/interest = 'uninteresting; boring; dull'

意 意 意 意 意 意 意 意 意 意 意 意 意

意

思 (*sī*)

sī	Ancient Form	Modern Form
think; contemplate	思	思
yǒu yìsi		有意思

思 (*sī*) associates two components, both of which you've seen before. The bottom is 心 (*xīn*) and relates to the heart/mind. That's a good clue for our thinking about this character. The top component, 囟/田, is viewed by some as an altered form of 'brain,' which again suggests 'thinking.' Others see the top as a field divided for cultivation, suggesting for some that 'one does one's best thinking sitting in the field.' Take your pick of clues. This character is a combination not of radical plus phonetic but of two components, each contributing meaning. A useful compound forms when 思 combines with 想 (*xiǎng*), producing 思想 (*sīxiǎng*), meaning 'thought (system).'

毛泽东 (*Máo Zédōng*) 思想真有意思／没意思.

思 思 思 思 思 思
思 思 思

思

Unit 7

The sentences below are inspired by the contents of Unit 7 and contain most of the new characters required for writing as well as others. Read and reread until fluent, covering the English as you read. Then cover the English and try to reproduce the Chinese equivalents orally. Do this exercise before beginning to practice writing.

這是我的東西, 不是你的. 这是我的东西, 不是你的.	These are my things; not yours.
你怎麼這麼忙? 你怎么这么忙?	How come you are so busy?
我不冷也不熱. 我不冷也不热.	I'm neither cold nor hot.
吃飽了, 就覺得很累. 吃饱了, 就觉得很累.	After eating my fill, I feel tired.
太太沒回來, 我很著急. 太太没回来, 我很着急.	My wife has not returned; I'm worried.
我餓了, 可是不想吃飯. 我饿了, 可是不想吃饭.	I'm hungry but I don't feel like eating.
對不起我得走了, 再見. 对不起我得走了, 再见.	Excuse me, but I have to leave; goodbye.
弟弟學得不好, 爸爸很不高興. 弟弟学得不好, 爸爸很不高兴.	Younger brother is not doing well in his studies, and dad's very unhappy.
你最近怎麼樣? 好嗎? 你最近怎么样? 好吗?	How have you been recently? Well?
我姐姐跟他先生回來了. 我姐姐跟他先生回来了.	My older sister and her husband have returned.
累了嗎? —不累. 有點兒餓. 累了吗? —不累. 有点儿饿.	Are you tired? —No, I'm not. I'm a bit hungry.
你覺得冷嗎? 要不要喝點兒熱的? 你觉得冷吗? 要不要喝点儿热的?	Are you feeling cold? Would you like to drink something hot?

你是著急還是生氣? 你是着急还是生气?	Are you worried or angry?
吃飽了,就覺得很睏. 吃饱了,就觉得很困.	(As soon as) I eat my fill, I feel sleepy.

Can You Construct a Chinese Character?

方 (*fāng*), as an independent character, means 'square; four-sided' and forms part of many compounds. 方 also serves as a very reliable phonetic for many characters, combining with radicals to form new and varied meanings. Many words in spoken Chinese are pronounced *fang* (with one or another of the four tones) and, over the centuries, when it came about that a spoken word pronounced as *fang* had no character of its own, the Chinese language found a solution by simply adding another component to 方 (we now call this component a 'radical') to suggest new meanings, hoping that readers would link sound and meaning clues and arrive at the meaning. Now it's your turn. With your knowledge of the radicals we have learned so far, plus one or two new ones below, you try now to create characters, all pronounced *fang* (with different tones) by adding an appropriate radical to suggest a particular meaning. Work with a friend.

Here are your radical choices:

wood	woman	sun	step	silk	word	person	grass	metal	earth
木	女	日	彳	纟	言/讠	亻/人	艹	金 / 钅	土

Which radical would you add to 方 to create the meanings below?

fang meaning 'bright dawn'

fang meaning 'a kind of tree; a long thick piece of lumber'

fang meaning 'a workshop; a mill; lane (part of a street name)'

fang meaning 'to call on someone; to visit someone'

fang meaning 'a pot, pan; wine vessel'

fang meaning 'sweet-smelling, fragrant'

fang meaning 'to imitate' (someone or something)

pang meaning 'walk back and forth'

fang meaning 'to spin' (cloth, silk, etc.)

fang meaning 'to obstruct; hinder; hamper' (*This one will really throw you a curve!*)

(*Answers on the next page.*)

Answers:

fāng, meaning 'bright dawn'	昉 (with the 'sun' radical)
fāng, meaning 'a kind of tree; a long, thick piece of lumber'	枋 (with the 'tree/wood' radical)
fāng, meaning 'a workshop; a mill; lane' (part of a street name)	坊 (with the 'land/earth' radical)
fǎng, meaning 'to call on someone; to visit someone'	訪/访 (with the 'speech' radical)
fāng, meaning 'a pot, pan; wine vessel'	鈁/钫 (with the 'metal' radical)
fāng, meaning 'sweet-smelling, fragrant'	芳 (with the 'grass' radical)
fǎng, meaning 'to imitate' (someone or something)	仿 (with the 'man/person' radical)
páng, meaning 'walk back and forth'	彷 (with the 'step/walk' radical)
fǎng, meaning 'to spin' (cloth, silk, etc.)	纺/紡 (with the 'silk' radical)
fáng, meaning 'to obstruct, hinder, hamper'	妨 (with the 'woman' radical)

I wish that all phonetic clues were as reliable as 方, but unfortunately, they are not. However, the more you are aware of them, the more attention you pay to them, the more useful they will become in your future Chinese language learning.

坐 (*zuò*)

zuò	Ancient Form	Modern Form
to sit; travel by	坐 (ancient form)	坐
qǐng zuò		請坐 / 请坐

The ancient form of 坐 is like a sketch of two men sitting on earth facing each other. The modern form has two 人 (*rén*, 'person') with 土 (*tǔ*, 'earth, land') in the middle. 坐 appears in compound words relating to 'sit' or 'take a bus/flight/train.' For example:

坐地铁 sit + subway = 'take the subway'	請坐 / 请坐 ask + sit = 'please take a seat'

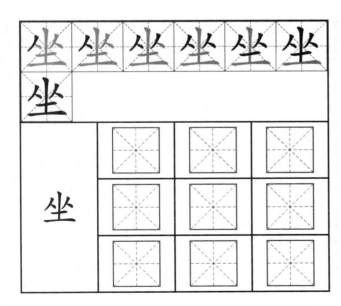

走 (zǒu)

zǒu	Ancient Form	Later Form	Modern Form
walk; leave; go	大	走	走
wǒ yào zǒu le			我要走了

The original meaning of 走 (*zǒu*) is 'to walk,' seen easily in the ancient form, a figure of a man with two swinging arms. Did the original picture go astray by adding detail? Well, the later form adds 止, the radical for 'foot,' on the bottom. Move your feet and walk and leave.

對不起, 我得走了. 　　—我也走了. 你去哪兒? 回家.	对不起, 我得走了. 　　—我也走了. 你去哪儿? 回家.

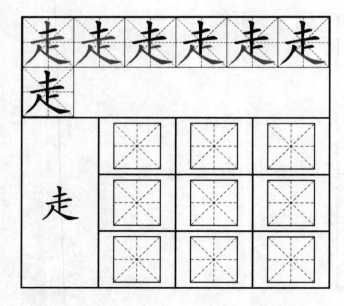

Copyright © 2012 by Yale University and China International Publishing Group

回 (*húi*)

húi	Ancient Form	Modern Form
return (to a place)	@	回
huílai		回來 / 回来

The character 回 (*hui*) is a pictograph of swirling water within an enclosure, curiously without the 'water' radical. You've seen the 'enclosure' radical before in *guó* 國/国. Notice how, in the ancient form, the line proceeds to the middle and then returns to the place where it was before, which is the basic meaning of 回.

我姐姐回來了. 我叫我弟弟早回來. 他還沒回來.	我姐姐回来了. 我叫我弟弟早回来. 他还没回来.
回家 go back + home = 'return to one's home'	回來 / 回来 turn back + come = 'come back; return'
回去 go back + go = 'go back' (to where one was)	回國 / 回国 return + country = 'return to one's native country'

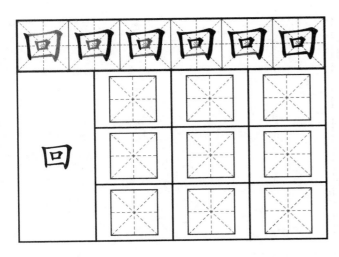

吃 (chī)

chī	Ancient Form	Modern Form
eat	吃	吃
chī fàn		吃飯 / 吃饭

吃 (*chī*) very logically adopts 口 ('mouth') as the radical, providing a good link since the character means 'eat' and is a picto-phonetic character. The right part is the phonetic component, but it is of little help. The right side means 'beg,' beg for food, and is pronounced *qī*. *qī > qī > qī > chī*. A pronunciation leap, yes, maybe even a broad jump, but it's the kind of link we have to make often in learning Chinese. 吃 is very productive of compounds. Here's just a few:

吃飯 / 吃饭	好吃	吃飽了 / 吃饱了	吃不下了	小吃
eat	delicious	eat to fullness	can't eat anymore	snack

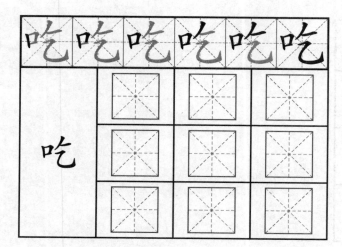

東/东 (dōng)

dōng	Ancient Form	Later Form	Modern Traditional Form	Modern Simplified Form
thing; some-thing; east	東	東	東	东
dōngxi			東西	东西

東/东 (dōng) is a combination character—that is, composed of two parts—but each intertwined rather than standing side by side or on top of one another. Look closely at the traditional form of 東 and you perhaps can isolate 日 (*rì*, 'sun') (a bit flattened), overlaying 木 (*mù*, 'tree'), which makes for a good recall aid, at least for the meaning 'east'—'sun rising behind the trees in the east.' But how about 東西/东西 (*dōngxi*, 'thing'), a compound word composed of 'east' and 'west'? Out of the east come many things for our use and pleasure, including the Chinese language. The simplified form, 东, has eliminated the 'sun' but at least has retained the 木 (*mù*, 'tree'). Distinguish 东 from its look-alike, the simplified character for 'vehicle,' 车 (*chē*).

我們去吃點兒東西, 好不好? 　—不行, 不能去, 有事.	我们去吃点儿东西, 好不好? 　—不行, 不能去, 有事.

Modern Traditional Form	Modern Simplified Form
東 東 東 東 東 東 東 東	东 东 东 东 东

西 (xī)

xī	Ancient Form	Later Form	Modern Form
west (*1st tone*); (*neutral tone in* dōngxi)	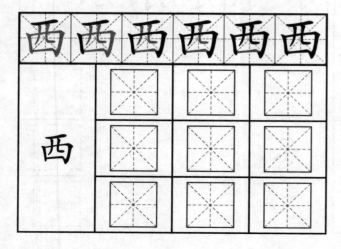		西
dōngxi			東西 / 东西

The early forms of 西 (*xī*) show a bird roosting, suggesting sunset and the direction 'west.' When the bird gets back to the nest, the sun is setting in the west. For our purposes, 西 (neutral tone) appears in *dōngxi* 東西 / 东西, meaning 'thing.' From east to west, one can find many things of interest.

Distinguish 西 from 要.

這些東西是你的嗎? —不是我的.	这些东西是你的吗? —不是我的.
西天 west + sky / day = 'Western Paradise' (the Buddhist heaven)	西方 west + side / direction = 'the West; Occident'
西南 west + south = 'southwest'	西德 west + Germany = 'West Germany'

西 西 西 西 西 西

西

吧 (ba)

ba	Ancient Form	Modern Form
(sentence-ending particle used in imperatives and suggestions [neutral tone])	吧	吧
Wǒmen zǒu ba!		我们走吧!

We are hoping that 吧 (*ba*) suggests another character to you. Does 吧 remind you of its look-alike 爸 (*bà*, 'father, dad')? In both, notice the common and useful phonetic 巴. 巴, paired with the now familiar 口 (*kǒu*), which signifies 'something oral,' such as a command or a suggestion. Do you recall any other characters compounded with the radical 口?

- 走吧! Let's go!
- 你還好吧? / 你还好吧? ('You're still okay, right?')

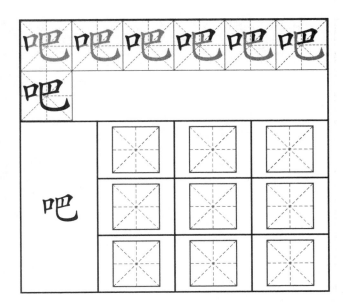

怎 (zěn)

zěn	Ancient Form	Modern Form
how?; what?; why?	㞉	怎
Zěnme?		怎麼 / 怎么

怎 (zěn) has 乍 (zuò) on top, which is the phonetic component. 心 (xīn) on the bottom is the signific component because when you ask 'how,' 'what,' or 'why,' your question comes from the heart.

你媽媽怎麼樣?	你妈妈怎么样?
你怎麼學中文?	你怎么学中文?
看看我怎麼寫.	看看我怎么写.
怎麼去?	怎么去?
你怎麼這麼忙?	你怎么这么忙?

Distinguish 怎 from 昨 (天) and (工) 作, all of which have the same phonetic 乍 (zuò).

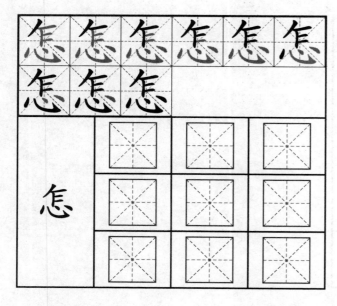

樣/样 (*yàng*)

yàng	Ancient Form	Modern Traditional Form	Modern Simplified Form
appearance; kind; shape	樣	樣	样
Zénme yàng?		怎麼樣?	怎么样?

樣/样 (*yàng*) gives us a lot. There's 木 ('tree') on the left; the bottom right looks like 水 'water' or 永 (*yǒng*, 'eternal'); above that is 羊 (*yáng*, 'sheep'). We have lots to remember and, perhaps, lots to help our recall. The simplified form simplifies things to a combination of 'tree' and 'sheep.' Trees are all of different shapes, sizes, and appearances. 羕/羊 (*yáng*, 'goat') on the right is the phonetic component. Goats come in different kinds as well.

一樣／一样 one + appearance = 'same'	同樣／同样 same + appearance/kind = 'same'
樣書／样书 mode/kind + book = 'sample book'	怎麼樣?／怎么样? how + appearance/kind = 'how's it going?'

Modern Traditional Form	Modern Simplified Form
樣 樣 樣 樣 樣 樣 樣 樣 樣 樣 樣 樣 樣 樣 樣	样 样 样 样 样 样 样 样 样 样
樣	样

高 (gāo)

gāo	Ancient Form	Later Form	Modern Form
tall; high (in *gāoxìng*, 'pleased; in high spirits')	髙	高	高
gāoxìng			高興／高兴

高 (gāo) seems to say 'high' all by itself, layer upon layer, reaching high into the sky. It is actually a sketch of a pavilion, a much favored and well loved 'high-rise' building in China.

你怎麼這麼高興？ 　—我兒子回來了, 所以很高興.	你怎么这么高兴？ 　—我儿子回来了, 所以很高兴.
高大 high/tall + big = 'tall and big'	高興／高兴 high/tall + excitement = 'happy'
高中 high + middle = 'senior high school'	高明 high + bright = 'clever; brilliant'

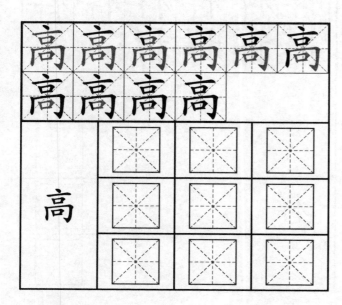

興/兴 (*xìng*)

xìng	Ancient Form	Later Form	Modern Traditional Form	Modern Simplified Form
excitement; interest	興	興	興	兴
gāoxìng			高興	高兴

"All hands on deck!" Do you see the 'hands' on both sides of 同 (*tóng*, 'same') in the early forms and the modern traditional form? 'All hands together' produces 'excitement' and 'high (高 *gāo*) enthusiasm,' which also gives rise to our 'having interest' 有興趣/有兴趣 (*yǒu xìngqù*). 興 has been really altered in the simplification process leaving not much for our recall. By the way, 有興趣/有兴趣 is a verb constructed with 有 (*yǒu*), so it's negated with 没 (*méi*), of course, e.g., 没(有)興趣 / 没(有)兴趣.

Modern Traditional Form	Modern Simplified Form

著/着 (zháo)

zháo	Ancient Form	Modern Traditional Form	Modern Simplified Form
feel	𧆘	著	着
zháojí		著急	着急

著/着 (zháo) compounds into 著急/着急 (*zháojí*, 'to feel anxiety' > 'be worried'). Notice 日 ('sun') at the bottom in the traditional form; the simplified form abandons 日 in favor of 目 ('eye'). The top part of the traditional form is the radical for 'plant' with 者 (*zhě*) beneath (remember 或者?); 者 is gone in the simplified form. Remember to keep simplified 着 distinct from your old friend 看 (*kàn*).

Modern Traditional Form
著 著 著 著 著 著
著 著 著 著 著 著
著

Modern Simplified Form
着 着 着 着 着 着
着 着 着 着 着 着
着

急 (jí)

jí	Ancient Form	Modern Form
anxious; worried	急	急
zháojí		著急 / 着急

急 (*jí*) has a familiar radical. Can you find it? It is 心 ('heart/mind'), right there at the bottom. When you're worried or anxious, your 'mind' is what is troubled. The 'heart/mind' is clearly visible in the ancient form. 及 (*jí*), on the top, is the phonetic component, but it has been considerably altered in its modern form. 及, meaning 'reach; attain,' also contributes to meaning. 'Get to where you stop worrying.'

你為甚麼這麼著急? —我女兒還沒回來, 我很著急.	你为什么这么着急? —我女儿还没回来, 我很着急.
着急 feel + anxious = 'worried; anxious'	急忙 anxious + busy = 'in great rush; hurried'
急事 anxious + matter = 'emergency'	急電 / 急电 anxious + electricity/telegram = 'urgent telegram (cable)'

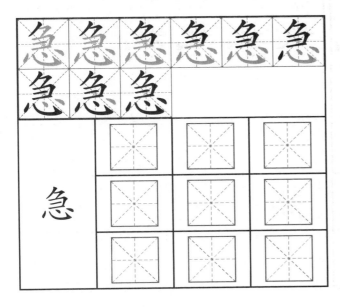

熱／热 (*rè*)

rè	Ancient Form	Modern Traditional Form	Modern Simplified Form
hot	𤇾	熱	热
rè shuǐ		熱水	热水

熱／热 (*rè*) has at its bottom a familiar radical that links well to its meaning. The radical is 火, but it is often altered into four dots (灬) when it is a character component. 埶／执 (*zhí*) on top is the unreliable phonetic component. By extension, 熱／热 also means 'ardent, warm,' as in 熱愛／热爱 (*rè'ài*, 'to love dearly'). Does the 九 part with a line through it look like an 'r'? 'r' for *re*?

熱心／热心 hot + heart = 'enthusiastic; warmhearted'	熱天／热天 hot + day = 'hot weather'
熱水／热水 hot + water = 'hot water'	熱中／热中 hot + among = 'be fond of'

Modern Traditional Form	Modern Simplified Form
熱 熱 熱 熱 熱 熱	热 热 热 热 热 热
熱 熱 熱 熱 熱 熱	热 热 热 热
熱 熱 熱	
熱	热

lěng	Ancient Form	Modern Form
cold; cool		冷
lěng shuǐ		冷水

冷 (*lěng*) is a picto-phonetic character. The radical, new to us, is 冫 ('ice'), two strokes, which looks something like the familiar radical 氵 (*shuǐ*, 'water'), which has three strokes. The right side, 令, is the phonetic, but it is pronounced *lìng*, so there is little help there. Keep 冷 and 今 (*jīn*, 'today') separate.

冷水 cold + water = 'cold water; unboiled water'	冷天 cold + day = 'cold (weather) day'
冷色 cool + color = 'cool colors' (white, green, blue—colors that make you feel cool)	冷氣/冷气 cold + air = 'air conditioning'

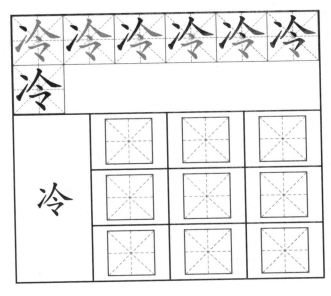

累 (*lèi*)

lèi	Ancient Form	Modern Form
tired; weary	畾系	累
Wǒ lèi le.		我累了.

累 (*lèi*) is a top-bottom character in which both components support its meaning. The top component we've seen before. Remember 男 (*nán*)? I regard the top, 田 (*tián*), as 'farming fields' whose furrows are clearly demarcated. The bottom, 系 (*sī*), is 'silk thread.' Farming and silk production are both labor intensive, and very tiring, so we've got our memory aid.

• 我一吃飯就覺得很累. • 這件事真累人. (累人, *lèi rén*, 'makes one tired') • 你累不累?—不累, 不累.	• 我一吃饭就觉得很累. • 这件事真累人. (累人, *lèi rén*, 'makes one tired') • 你累不累?—不累, 不累.

累 累 累 累 累 累
累 累 累 累 累

累

忙 (*máng*)

máng	Ancient Form	Modern Form
busy	忄亡	忙
tài máng le		太忙了

Get ready for a bonus on this one. Take a look at these two characters: 忙 and 忘. Exactly the same components, in each case an amalgam of a 心 ('sitting heart/mind') or a 忄 ('standing heart/mind'), combined with the pretty good phonetic 亡 (*wáng*), which also contributes some meaning. 亡 means 'lost.' So:

忙 (*máng*, 'busy'): I'm so busy I'm losing my mind!
忘了 (*wàng*, 'forget'): I've lost track of something—i.e., forgotten it.

Examples:
我不能去, 太忙了。
我又忙又累。
忙不忙? —真忙, 真忙.

Bonus:

我忘了她叫甚麼名字.	我忘了她叫什么名字.

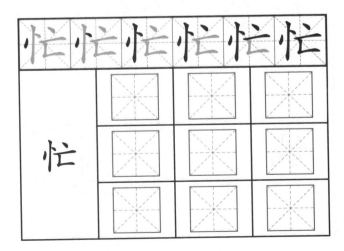

餓/饿 (è)

è	Ancient Form	Modern Traditional Form	Modern Simplified Form
hungry	餓	餓	饿
Wǒ è le.		我餓了.	我饿了.

With the arrival of 餓/饿 (è), we have some good news. Both components should be familiar to you. On the left side is 食/饣 ('food'). The right part is 我 (*wǒ*, 'I; me'), so the character presents 'I eat.' When do we eat? When we're hungry, of course. By the way, it turns out that the ancient pronunciation of 我 was very similar to è, but over the centuries e (*uh*) changed into *wǒ* (*woh*). 我 is thus both the signific and phonetic component. Remember to keep 餓 distinct from the 俄 (*é*) in 俄國/俄国 (*Éguó*, 'Russia').

我有點兒餓, 你餓了嗎? ——不餓, 不餓, 有點兒渴. (*kě*, 'thirsty')	我有点儿饿, 你饿了吗? ——不饿不饿, 有点儿渴. (*kě*, 'thirsty')

Modern Traditional Form	Modern Simplified Form
餓 餓 餓 餓 餓 餓 餓 餓 餓 餓 餓 餓 餓 餓 餓	饿 饿 饿 饿 饿 饿 饿 饿 饿 饿
餓	饿

飯/饭 (*fàn*)

fàn	Ancient Form	Modern Traditional Form	Modern Simplified Form
meal; cooked rice	䭫	飯	饭
chī fàn		吃飯	吃饭

飯/饭 (*fàn*) is a model radical-plus-phonetic character. On the left, the typical place for the radical, is 食/饣 ('food'), while on the right, 反 (*fǎn*) provides the phonetic component, a very reliable one, except for the tone, of course. What's more, the simplification process has not tampered with the structure, except for making the radical contain fewer strokes. Here's some compounds using 飯/饭 and their meanings. Can you match each compound with its correct meaning?

早飯	中飯	午飯	晚飯	米飯	飯館	吃飯	要飯	白飯
eat a meal	restaurant	dinner	to beg for food	lunch	white rice	lunch	breakfast	cooked rice

Modern Traditional Form	Modern Simplified Form
飯 飯 飯 飯 飯 飯 飯 飯 飯 飯 飯 飯	饭 饭 饭 饭 饭 饭

bǎo	Ancient Form	Later Form	Modern Traditional Form	Modern Simplified Form
full (as in eating)			飽	饱
chībǎo le			吃飽了	吃饱了

The ancient form of this character, as is somewhat evident above, is a person leaning/bending over a display of food, eating until full, satisfied, satiated. The later form and the modern forms are picto-phonetic characters. The left part, 食/饣, is the radical-signific component, meaning 'food.' The right part, 包 (bāo), is the very reliable phonetic component, worth learning in itself, for its occurrence in the 'delicious' word 包子 (bāozi, 'Chinese dumplings'), one of my favorite treats. When I start eating bāozi, I keep going until I'm full!

我吃飽了，不能再吃了.	我吃饱了，不能再吃了.

Modern Traditional Form	Modern Simplified Form
飽 飽 飽 飽 飽 飽 飽 飽 飽 飽 飽 飽 飽	饱 饱 饱 饱 饱 饱 饱 饱

飽			

饱			

Unit 8

The sentences below are inspired by the contents of Unit 8 and contain nearly all the new characters required for writing as well as others. Read and reread until fluent, covering the English as you read. Then cover the English and try to reproduce the Chinese equivalents orally. Do this exercise before beginning to practice writing and afterward.

我每週吃三次中國飯。 我每周吃三次中国饭。	I eat 'Chinese' three times per week.
你這個週末想到哪兒去玩兒？ 你这个周末想到哪儿去玩儿？	Where do you want to go for some fun this weekend?
你出去玩兒以前得先洗臉洗手。 你出去玩儿以前得先洗脸洗手。	Before you go out to play you must first wash your hands and face.
中國人常説早睡早起身體好。 中国人常说早睡早起身体好。	Chinese people often say 'early to bed, early to rise, is good for health.'
我昨天晚上睡覺睡得不好。 我昨天晚上睡觉睡得不好。	I didn't sleep well last night.
每天呆在家裡上網看電視不行。 每天呆在家里上网看电视不行。	It won't do to stay at home and go on-line and watch television every day.
你從中國回來以後想做甚麼？ 你从中国回来以后想做什么？	After you return from China, what do you plan to do?
每天上班下班我覺得沒意思。 每天上班下班我觉得没意思。	It's no fun (just) going to work and coming home from work every day.
你出門以前別忘了洗個澡。 你出门以前别忘了洗个澡。	Before you leave don't forget to take a bath. (*Note the dropping of 一 before the measure word; often seen in Chinese.*)

Further Practice with Radicals

Below is a selection of characters introduced in Units 6, 7, and 8. Working with a partner if possible, circle the radical in each, recall the meaning, provide a compound or phrase in pinyin or, better still, in characters, and, finally, formulate a connection between radical and character meaning. Notice how the original radical in the traditional form has disappeared in the simplification process in some cases. What effect has such 'disappearance' had on your memory aid?

做	累
想	忙
要	怎
念	吃
级/級	急
思	飯/饭
賺/赚	洗
還/还	看
她	網/网
道	睡
热/熱	週/周

週/周 (*zhōu*)

zhōu	Ancient Form	Later Form	Modern Traditional Form	Modern Simplified Form
cycle (*of time*); week	周	周	週	周
zhōumò			週末	周末

From the ancient form of *zhōu* 週/周, we can understand that it originally meant 'the boundary line of a figure, area, or object.' 週 (*zhōu*), in its modern traditional form, takes 辶, the 'movement' radical, and that associates well with 'cycle'—a time cycle; a week. Add 末 (*mò*, 'end') to get 週末/周末 (*zhōumò*, weekend). For interest's sake, notice the 口 ('mouth') inside 週/周 and 土 (*tǔ*, 'land, ground') above the 口. Any associations there?

週末來了, 不用上班, 我們出去玩吧!	周末来了, 不用上班, 我们出去玩吧!
週末到了, 可以睡懶覺了!	周末到了, 可以睡懒觉了!

週末/周末 a week + end = 'weekend'	週年/周年 a cycle + year = 'anniversary'
上週/上周 up/past + week = 'last week'	下週/下周 down/next + week = 'next week'

Modern Traditional Form	Modern Simplified Form
週 週 週 週 週 週	周 周 周 周 周 周
週 週 週 週 週 週	周 周

末 (mò)

mò	Ancient Forms	Modern Form
end	柰 柰	末
zhōumò		週末/周末

Look closely at 末 (*mò*) and you will see 木 (*mù*, 'wood'). 末 is a tree with a couple of branches at its top or its end. So, logically, the language uses 末 to indicate the end of a tree, or of a time period, such as a week (週末/周末) or the end of a semester (期末, *qīmò*). Distinguish 末 and 木.

週末的時候, 大家都可以出去玩兒.	周末的时候, 大家都可以出去玩儿.
週末完了以後, 大家都得上班工作.	周末完了以后, 大家都得上班工作.
週末來了以後, 我覺得很高興.	周末来了以后 我觉得很高兴.

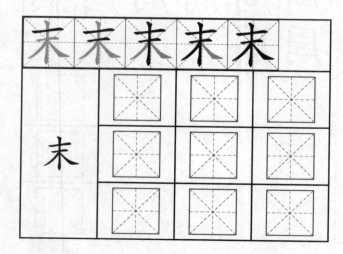

睡 (*shuì*)

shuì	Ancient Form	Modern Form
sleep; go to bed	睡	睡
shuìjiào		睡覺／睡觉

The character 睡 (*shuì*) returns us to basics: radical plus phonetic. The 目 (*mù*) radical on the left, the signific, means 'eye,' while the right side 垂 (*chuí*, 'droop') is the near phonetic. So 'eyes droop,' therefore 'sleep.' Okay, *chuí* is not *shuì*, but it's about as close as phonetic clues often get. I've always found the right side of 睡 a bit tough to write. I'm sure you'll have better success.

我是晚睡晚起, 你呢? —我是早睡早起.	我是晚睡晚起, 你呢? —我是早睡早起.
早睡早起, 身體好.	早睡早起, 身体好.
睡覺／睡觉 to sleep + asleep = 'to sleep'	睡衣 to sleep + clothes = 'pajamas'
午睡 noon + sleep = 'noontime nap; have an afternoon nap'	睡懶覺／睡懒觉 to sleep + lazy + asleep = 'to sleep in'

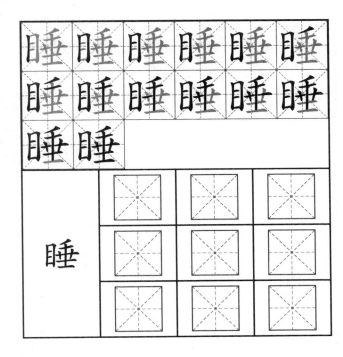

覺/觉 (*jiào*)

jiào	Ancient Form	Modern Traditional Form	Modern Simplified Form
sleep	覺	覺	觉
shuìjiào		睡覺	睡觉

We could learn a lot from 覺/觉 (*jiào*), but the clues are a bit confusing. 覺 combines 'see' (見/见) and a reduced part of 'study' (學, *xué*). 'See' + 'study' = 'sleep'? Well, let's not go there, okay? 覺/觉 has two pronunciations: *jiào* and *jué*, the former meaning 'sleep' and the latter meaning 'sense; feel' or 'become aware,' and forms part of the compound 覺得/觉得 (*juéde*, 'feel'), which we have seen before.

你早上幾點起床, 晚上幾點睡覺? 　　—早上很晚起床, 晚上很晚睡覺. 那不好, 早睡早起身體好.	你早上几点起床, 晚上几点睡觉? 　　—早上很晚起床, 晚上很晚睡觉. 那不好, 早睡早起身体好.
睡覺/睡觉 to sleep + asleep = 'to sleep'	午覺/午觉 noon + asleep = 'afternoon nap'
睡懶覺/睡懒觉 to sleep + lazy + asleep = 　'to sleep in'	你覺得怎麼樣? 你觉得怎么样? 'How do 　you feel? What do you think?'

Modern Traditional Form	Modern Simplified Form
覺 覺 覺 覺 覺 覺 覺 覺 覺 覺 覺 覺 覺 覺 覺 覺 覺 覺 覺 覺	觉 觉 觉 觉 觉 觉 觉 觉 觉
覺	觉

看 (kàn)

kàn	Ancient Form	Modern Form
look; watch; read	睂	看
kàn shū		看書 / 看书

看 (*kàn*) combines 手 (*shǒu*, 'hand' [a bit distorted]) on top and 目 (*mù*, 'eye') on the bottom. Now you need both hand and eye to 'read,' so maybe that's a clue worth considering. 看 originally meant 'look from a distance,' so the meanings 'watch; see' come into play as well. Here are some useful compounds featuring 看:

看書	看懂	看見	看看	看電影	看電視	看朋友	看法
看书	看懂	看见	看看	看电影	看电视	看朋友	看法

看法 = 'viewpoint, perspective'; remember: distinguish 看 and 着—e.g., 着急 (*zháojí*, 'worried').

電/电 (diàn)

diàn	Ancient Form	Modern Traditional Form	Modern Simplified Form
electricity	電	電	电
diànshì		電視	电视

Benjamin Franklin would have loved this character. 電/电 (*diàn*) is a picture of lightning and therefore 'electricity/electric,' and it communicates meaning to us with both its components. In keeping with its original meaning of 'lightning,' the top part is 雨 (*yǔ*, 'rain'), and we all know what's often hidden in dark clouds. The bottom part depicts a bolt of lightning striking the land, 田 (*tián*), which the simplified form thankfully preserves. Recall: Ben Franklin.

週末來了, 我們去看電影, 好嗎? 　—我不能去看電影, 太忙了.	周末来了, 我们去看电影, 好吗? 　—我不能去看电影, 太忙了.
電影 / 电影 electric + shadow = 'movie'	電視 / 电视 electric + watch/sight = 'television'
電子 / 电子 electricity + *word suffix* = 'electron'	電話 / 电话 electric + words = 'telephone'

Modern Traditional Form	Modern Simplified Form
電 電 電 電 電 電 電 電 電 電 電 電 電	电 电 电 电 电
電	电

視/视 (*shì*)

shì	Ancient Form	Modern Traditional Form	Modern Simplified Form
see; watch	視	視	视
diànshì		電視	电视

It's so good to see in a new character a component you've seen before. In 視/视 (*shì*) you see an old friend, 見/见 (*jiàn*) (看見/看见), and 見/见 ('see, watch') offers a good memory clue for us, since our relevant word is television (*diànshì*). The left side is a 'table,' on which the television or anything else stands. Review these old friends, 現/现 and 裡/里, both of which have components present in 視/视.

我今天要在家裡看電視. 　—呆在家裡不好, 出去玩吧! 可是今天的電視節目很好. 　—電視上沒有好節目.	我今天要在家里看电视. 　—呆在家里不好, 出去玩吧! 可是今天的电视节目很好. 　—电视上没有好节目.

(節目 / 节目 *jiémù* 'program')

Modern Traditional Form	Modern Simplified Form
視 視 視 視 視 視 視 視 視 視 視	视 视 视 视 视 视 视 视
視	视

影 (*yǐng*)

yǐng	Ancient Form	Modern Form
shadow; reflection	景	影
diànyǐng ('movie')		電影 / 电影

The character 影 (*yǐng*) offers many clues. For pronunciation, I always notice the 京 (*jīng*) on the bottom left and recall my favorite place in the world: 北京 (*Běijīng*). On the right side, we find 彡, a form new to us and rather unusual. In some characters, 彡 means 'sun's rays' (which cast shadows, of course), while in other characters, 彡 seems to indicate 'hairs' or 'fine feathers.' Your job? Connect one or more of these clues with 'shadow' and then get yourself to a movie.

我覺得看電影很有意思. —看電影沒意思. 我喜歡玩電子遊戲.	我觉得看电影很有意思. —看电影没意思. 我喜欢玩电子游戏.
電影 / 电影 electricity + shadow = 'movie'	影星 shadow + star = 'movie star'

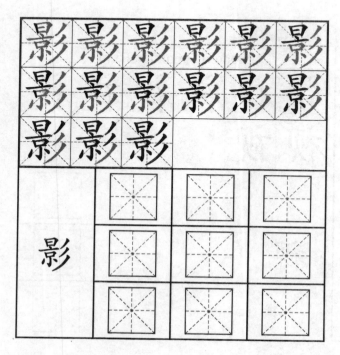

wán	Ancient Form	Modern Form
to play	玩	玩
chūqù wán(r)		出去玩儿

The two components of 玩 (*wán*) are familiar friends. On the left is 玉, 'jade,' but it is often altered into 王 with the result that it looks identical to 王 (*wáng*, 'king'). Remember the simplified character 国 (*guó*, 'nation; country')? There you see the 玉 ('jade'). Now why is 'jade' associated with 'play'? It is because the original meaning of 玩 is 'to play with jade.' The right side should be familiar as well. It's 元 (*yuán*), the word for the basic Chinese monetary unit (e.g., 'yuan,' 'dollar') used in written prices all the time. 元 also supplies the near phonetic. The *ér* 兒/儿 ending to *wánr* 玩 in speech is very common. Distinguish: 玩, 元, and 完 (e.g., 做完, 'to finish').

明天你到我家來玩兒，好不好？ 　—玩兒甚麼？幾點去？ 玩兒電子遊戲，做完功課就來。 　—好啊！	明天你到我家来玩儿，好不好？ 　—玩儿什么？几点去？ 玩儿电子游戏，做玩功课就来。 　—好啊！

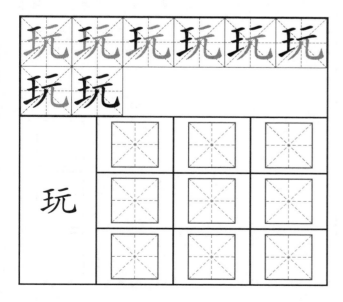

wǎng	Ancient Form	Later Form	Modern Traditional Form	Modern Simplified Form
net	𦥑	𠕎	網	网
shàng wǎng			上網	上网

The ancient form and the modern simplified form of 网 (*wǎng*) are remarkably similar. Both just look like a net. The simplified form has dispensed with 糸, the 'silk cloth/thread' radical present on the left side in the traditional form, but the 'thread' component—which, in my view, is the stuff of nets—is a good reminder of the meaning.

你天天上網不行, 也得看書.	你天天上网不行, 也得看书.
我不懂怎麼上網, 你幫我, 好嗎?	我不懂怎么上网, 你帮我, 好吗?
網球 / 网球 net + ball = 'tennis'	上網 / 上网 go to + net = 'go on the Internet; go online'

Modern Traditional Form	Modern Simplified Form
網 網 網 網 網 網 網 網 網 網 網 網 網 網	网 网 网 网 网 网
網	网

mén	Ancient Form	Later Form	Modern Traditional Form	Modern Simplified Form
door; gate	門	門	門	门
chū mén			出門	出门

If 門/门 (*mén*) is not a picture that is suggestive of a door with leaves, I don't know what is. Since I like classic Western movies, I think of the swinging doors leading into the ever present saloon in the middle of a Wild West town. Be sure to distinguish these look-alikes: 們/们, 門/门.

你早上幾點出門? 　—我六點半出門. 你呢? 我十點才出門, 比你晚得多.	你早上几点出门? 　—我六点半出门. 你呢? 我十点才出门, 比你晚得多.
天安門 / 天安门 heaven + peace + gate = 　'Gate of Heavenly Peace' (in Beijing)	門口 / 门口 door + mouth = 'doorway, 　entrance; gateway'
後門 / 后门 back/later + door = 'backdoor; 　backdoor influence'	大門 / 大门 large + door = 'main door'

Modern Traditional Form	Modern Simplified Form
門 門 門 門 門 門 門 門	门 门 门
門	门

以 (yǐ)

yǐ	Ancient Form	Later Form	Modern Form
(used before certain words of time and position)			以
yǐqián ('before') *yǐhòu* ('after; later')			以前 以後 / 以后

以 can mean 'to use; by means of,' as you might be able to guess from the ancient form. As a beginning student of Chinese, you will run into 以 (*yǐ*) in the context of a compound. I have no memory aid to offer for this character except context. You will see it in 以前 ('before'), 以後 / 以后 ('after; later'), 以上 ('above'), 以下 ('below'), 所以 ('because'), and so on. As we have said before, context is your best friend when reading—or, in fact, doing anything with language.

晚飯以後, 我們出去走走好不好?	晚饭以后, 我们出去走走, 好不好?
你睡覺以前別忘了洗個澡!	你睡觉以前别忘了洗个澡!
你不去, 所以我也不去.	你不去, 所以我也不去.

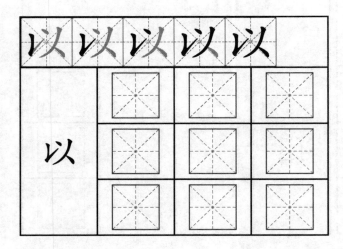

以

qián	Ancient Form	Modern Form
preceding; before; front	肯	前
yǐqián		以前

Analysis of character components will, in the overwhelming majority of cases, help your memory. As you've learned, such analysis takes effort and study. In the case of this character, 前 (*qián*, 'front'), however, the components do not seem to yield much. My solution? The surrounding contextual characters, like 以 (*yǐ*) (i.e., 以前), like 年 (*nián*) (i.e., 前年), can help recall. Remember: Context, context, context—a good reading strategy to employ whenever you read. It never fails to help.

吃飯以前別忘了洗個手. 睡覺以前別忘了洗個澡. 出去玩以前別忘了做功課.	吃饭以前别忘了洗个手. 睡觉以前别忘了洗个澡. 出去玩以前别忘了做功课.
前面 front + side = 'in front; front of'	前頭 / 前头 front + head = 'front; front of'
前天 before + day = 'the day before yesterday'	前年 preceding + year = 'year before last'

前 前 前 前 前 前
前 前 前

前

後/后 (hòu)

hòu	Ancient Form	Later Form	Modern Traditional Form	Modern Simplified Form
later; afterwards	後	後	後	后
yǐhòu			以後	以后

In the ancient form and the later form, the left part is 彳, an important radical meaning 'small steps.' You've seen it before. Can you identify these four 'look-alikes': 很, 得, 从, and 往? Well, if you take 'small steps,' you will certainly lag behind or even be left behind and will have to catch up later. The modern simplified form, 后, is a phonetic loan, the result of a process in which a seldom-used character is borrowed and used for a common word with the same pronunciation—in this case, hòu, 'empress.'

起床以後	吃飯以後	洗臉刷牙以後	來了以後	跑步以後	上班以後
起床以后	吃饭以后	洗脸刷牙以后	来了以后	跑步以后	上班以后

後門/后门 back/behind + door = 'back-door; backdoor influence'	最後/最后 most + later = 'finally'

Modern Traditional Form	Modern Simplified Form
後 後 後 後 後 後 後 後 後	后 后 后 后 后 后
後	后

洗 (xǐ)

xǐ	Ancient Form	Later Form	Modern Form
wash	洗	洗	洗
xǐ zǎo			洗澡

洗 (xǐ) is your typical radical-plus-phonetic character, the kind you can grow to love. On the left, as usual, is the radical, one familiar to you by now, 氵 (shuǐ; we've also encountered it in 没 and 法), while on the right is the phonetic 先 (xiān)—not quite xǐ, of course, but, again as usual, as close to the modern pronuncation as phonetics often get. The original meaning of this character was 'to wash one's foot,' as the ancient form seems to show, but later it came to mean 'to wash anything.'

你是早上洗澡還是晚上洗澡? —早晚都洗. 天天洗兩次澡.	你是早上洗澡还是晚上洗澡? —早晚都洗. 天天洗两次澡.
洗手 wash + hand = 'to wash (one's) hands'	洗手間 / 洗手间 wash + hand + (*measure word for*) room = 'lavatory, restroom'

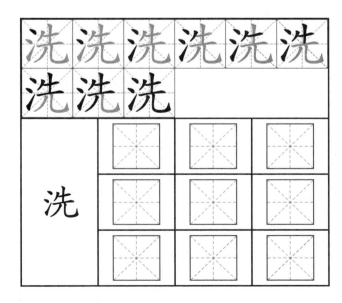

手 (shǒu)

shǒu	Ancient Form	Modern Form
hand	Ψ	手
xǐ shǒu		洗手

手 (shǒu) is a pictographic character, a picture of a 'hand.' A six-digit hand? Well, five or six, 手 is a very important radical relating to practically anything done with the hand. 手 is written as 扌 when it is a radical. Early forms of the character depicted a sketch of five fingers with the lower part of one's arm. Take a look at some common compounds using 手 just to review 'old' characters:

水手 ('sailor')	人手 ('manpower')	高手 ('expert')
新 (xīn) 手 ('novice')	親手 / 亲手 ('personally')	好手 ('expert')
生手 ('novice')	手法 ('skill')	手中 ('on hand; in possession of')

and a brand new one—手機 / 手机 (shǒujī, 'cell phone').

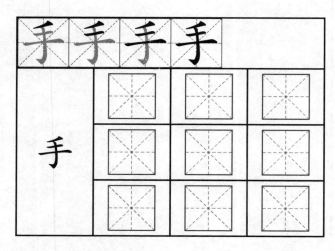

每 (*měi*)

měi	Ancient Form	Later Form	Modern Form
each; every; per	𡴌	𣫭	每
měi zhōu			每週／每周

Here's a bonus for you; a three-for-one deal. You already know 母 (*mǔ*) from 母親／母亲 (*mǔqīn*, 'mother'). Well, add a couple of stokes on the top and you get 每 (*měi*, 'each and every' [mother is wonderful]). Add three drops of water to 每 and you get 海—上海的海 ('the *hǎi* of Shanghai').

Distinguish 每 and 母 and 海.

我每次去上海, 他都請我吃晚飯.	他没次去上海, 他都请我吃晚饭.
他每年都去一次上海看他母親.	他每年都去一次上海看他母亲.
他每次都吃一次他母親做的上海菜.	他每次都吃一次他母亲做的上海菜.

每天 each/every + day = 'every day'	每次 each/every + (*measure word*) time = 'each time'
每個人／每个人 each/every + person = 'each/every person; everyone'	每年 each/every + year = 'each year'

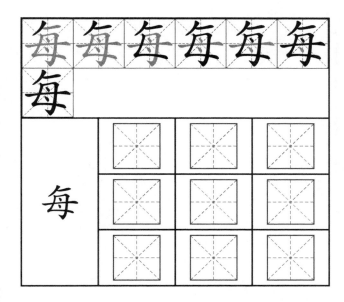

班 (*bān*)

bān	Ancient Form	Modern Form
shift (*of work*)	班	班
shàng bān, xià bān		上班, 下班

班 (*bān*) is formed by two pieces of 玉 (*yù*, 'jade' [altered]) and a 刀 ('knife' [altered]) in the middle. It originally meant 'to separate jade according to its quality.' As a memory aid, the altered 玉 (without the 'dot') can be read as 王 (*wáng*), meaning 'king.' Since we are trying to arrive at the meaning of 'work,' I like to take 王 as 'king' or even 'boss.' There you are at 'work' surrounded by 'bosses' who think themselves 'kings.'

爸爸, 你明天下班以後還有事嗎?	爸爸, 你明天下班以后还有事吗?
—下班以後沒事. 為甚麼問?	—下班以后没事. 为什么问?
下班以後, 想不想出去吃飯?	下班以后, 想不想出去吃饭?
—很想去. 好主意! (好主意, *hǎo zhǔyì*, 'good idea')	—很想去. 好主意! (好主意, *hǎo zhǔyì*, 'good idea')

Unit 9

The sentences below are inspired by the contents of Unit 9 and contain all the new characters required for writing as well as others. Read and reread until fluent, covering the English as you read. Then cover the English and try to reproduce the Chinese equivalents orally. Do this exercise before beginning to practice writing.

您貴姓? —我姓王, 叫王大山. 您贵姓? —我姓王, 叫王大山.	May I ask your name? —My name is Wang Dashan.
我很想做買賣, 做買賣可以賺錢. 我很想做买卖, 做买卖可以赚钱.	I really want to be in business; one can make money in business.
媽媽想給我買一件黑的, 一件白的. 妈妈想给我买一件黑的, 一件白的.	Mom intends to buy a black one and a white one for me.
我不喜歡穿紅的, 太不好看了! 我不喜欢穿红的, 太不好看了!	I don't like to wear red things; they're really ugly. (穿 = chuān, 'wear')
一百塊美元能換多少人民幣? 一百快美元能换多少人民币?	One hundred U.S. dollars can be exchanged for how much RMB?
我的錢不夠, 不能買. 你買好不好? 我的钱不够, 不能买. 你买好不好?	I don't have enough money; I can't buy it. You buy it, okay?
這件比那件便宜點兒, 最好買這件. 这件比那件便宜点儿, 最好买这件.	This one is cheaper than that one; you'd better buy this one.
金色的跟銀色的兩個都太貴, 我都不買. 金色的跟银色的两个都太贵, 我都不买.	Both the gold one and the silver one are too expensive; I'm not buying either.

Yes, You Can Type Chinese!

On either a Mac or a PC, after some practice, you can easily type Chinese characters. For the Mac we recommend going to the following website for information about setting up your computer to type in Chinese:

http://www.yale.edu/chinesemac/pages/input_methods.html

And for the PC go to:

http://www.pinyinjoe.com/

Once you have installed the necessary input software and selected your preferred form of the Chinese characters, traditional or simplified, you will type untoned pinyin, as in the following sentence: *wo you yi ge hao pengyou xing zhang* (in many input systems, you type the pinyin without the spaces between the words, e.g., *woyouyigepengyouxingzhang*). Most common characters, as you will see, appear correctly without your having to make choices from options. Type a correct spelling in pinyin and a character will appear. For the above sentence, the following characters will likely appear on your screen: 我有一个好朋友姓章.

The characters the software has chosen are correct, except the last one. You must recognize that 章 is not the correct choice. As you type *zhang* a list of choices will automatically appear, and you then need to make the correct choice by moving down the list with the arrow key and choosing the correct character, 張/张。Hit the space bar and the wrong character will then be replaced by the one you want. You have now typed a sentence in Chinese. Note that common compounds like *pengyou* can be typed as one word without spaces, but numbers and measure words like *yi ge* must be typed with separation (input systems that allow you to type a string of pinyin without spaces between the words do not have this requirement). These directions are very basic and may vary with the input software you use, but you will soon get the hang of it. It's fun and fast, and practice will make perfect.

Keep in mind that effective use of word processing for Chinese depends on correct choice of character options provided by the computer—that is, recognizing the character that you want. Such recognition skill is related to your overall competence in Chinese; your knowledge of structure, grammar, and vocabulary; and also your knowledge of writing, of character components, of radicals and phonetics, and so on. So far there's no 'Spelling and Grammar Check' available for Chinese word processing. You must provide your own checking. Typing accurately and fluently depends on your Chinese.

Have fun!

黑 (*hēi*)

hēi	Ancient Form	Later Form	Modern Form
black; dark	𡨄	𤎩	黑
hēisè			黑色

The character 黑 (*hēi*, 'black') has had more than one interpretation. Some liken the character to a chimney with the radical 'fire' appropriately at the bottom 'blackening' the chimney; another theory is that it depicts a window darkened by fire. Either way, something is turning black. Keep in mind that the radical is one you have seen before several times. It is 火 (*huǒ*, 'fire'), written with 'four licks of flame,' as 灬. Recall: 點/点 and see 'fire' and black in it.

天黑了，不能出去玩兒。	天黑了，不能出去玩儿。
黑色的太貴了，我不買。	黑色的太贵了，我不买。
黑白電視太不好看了。	黑白电视太不好看了。

黑白電視 / 黑白电视 black + white + television = 'black-and-white television'	黑色 black + color = 'black color'
黑海 black + sea = 'the Black Sea'	黑人 black + person = 'black person'

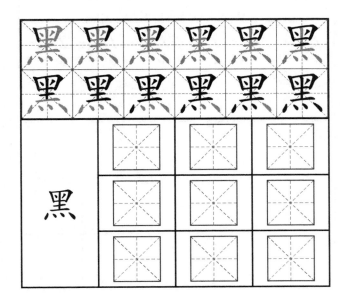

紅/红 (hóng)

hóng	Ancient Form	Modern Traditional Form	Modern Simplified Form
red	紅	紅	红
hóngsè		紅色	红色

紅/红 (hóng) provides a two-for-one opportunity. The left part, 糸/纟, is the radical/signific/meaning component, something to do with 'silk thread.' The right part, 工 (gōng), is the phonetic component, and it means 'work' or 'worker.' The 'worker' (工人 gōngrén) is producing red silk through his labor (工作 gōngzuò). gong, gong, gong > hong!

Review colors:

báide	hēide	lánde	jīnsède	huángde	kāfēisède	zǐsède
白的	黑的	藍的/蓝的	金色的	黃的	咖啡色的	紫色的

紅海/红海 red + sea = 'Red Sea'	口紅/口红 mouth + red = 'lipstick'
紅包/红包 red + package = (red envelope with money given to children at holiday time)	紅茶/红茶 red + tea = (what we call) 'black tea'!

Modern Traditional Form	Modern Simplified Form
紅 紅 紅 紅 紅 紅 紅 紅 紅	红 红 红 红 红 红
紅	红

白 (bái)

bái	Ancient Form	Later Form	Modern Form
white	⊖	白	白
báisè			白色

You've seen 白 (*bái*) before, at least part of it. Remember 日 (*rì*), a pictograph of the 'sun'? A stroke was added later, which I interpret as a sun flare, a sun spot, a ray from the sun, bringing white light to earth. The sun's actual color is white, although it appears yellow from the earth. Enough clues?

我要買一件白色的毛衣, 有嗎? 　—對不起沒有, 只有黑色的, 行嗎? 不是白色的, 不行.	我要买一件白色的毛衣, 有吗? 　—对不起没有, 只有黑色的, 行吗? 不是白色的, 不行.

黑白電視 / 黑白电视 black + white + television = 'black-and-white television'	白色 white + color = 'white in color'
白天 white + day = 'daytime'	白人 white + person = 'white person'

Note: The 'sunspot' is written downward and to the left.

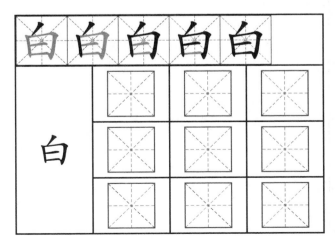

jīn	Ancient Form	Modern Form
gold; money		金
jīnsè		金色

Do you see a 'mountain' in 金 (*jīn*), right there on top, with 'nuggets' buried there in the 土 (*tǔ*, 'dirt')? Think of 'nuggets' of gold, meaning riches, gold, wealth. The top part is 今 (*jīn*), somewhat altered, to be sure, but there just the same, especially in the pre-modern form. 金 is an important radical; when it is a radical component, 金 is written 金 / 钅.

你覺得買甚麼東西最貴？ 　—當然買金子做的東西最貴． 買銀子做的東西也貴吧？ 　—對，可是沒有金子做的那麼貴．	你觉得买什么东西最贵？ 　—当然买金子做的东西最贵． 买银子做的东西也贵吧？ 　—对，可是没有金子做的那么贵．

現金 / 现金 current + gold = 'cash'	金黃 gold + yellow = 'golden yellow'
金錢 / 金钱 gold + money = 'money'	美金 U.S. + gold = 'American currency'

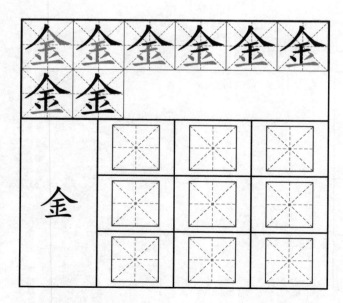

銀/银 (*yín*)

yín	Ancient Form	Modern Traditional Form	Modern Simplified Form
silver	銀	銀	银
yínsè		銀色	银色

Let's start with the phonetic this time and build some characters. Starting with 艮 (*gēn*), let's add the 'metal' radical on the left and get the above character, 銀/银 (*yín*). Let's add the radical 'step' and get 很 (*hěn*, 'very'). Let's add 'foot' and get 跟 (*gēn*, '[together] with'). Let's add 目 ('eye') and get 眼 (*yǎn*, 'eye'). Let's add 木 ('tree') and get 根 (*gēn*, 'basis; foundation'). Let's add 'heart' and get 恨 (*hèn*, 'hate'). This has been just for fun, but enough is enough. 够了, 够了!

先生您想買甚麼？ 　—有沒有銀子做的東西？ 對不起，沒有銀子做的東西，只有金子做的. 　—不行，我只要買銀子做的東西.那，我 　　走了.	先生您想买什么？ 　—有没有银子做的东西？ 对不起，没有银子做的东西，只有金子做的. 　—不行，我只要买银子做的东西.那，我 　　走了.

Modern Traditional Form	Modern Simplified Form
銀 銀 銀 銀 銀 銀 銀 銀 銀 銀 銀 銀 銀 銀	银 银 银 银 银 银 银 银 银 银 银
銀	银

元 (yuán)

yuán	Ancient Form	Later Form	Modern Simplified Form
Chinese monetary unit; dollar	𠄶	𠄶	元
Měi yuán			美元

The original meaning of 元 (yuán) was 'head,' and it therefore has extended meanings of 'first; primary; chief,' and so on. Later it was borrowed to serve as the primary unit of Chinese currency (and Japanese currency, by the way—the yen). The character 元 is a combination of 二 with 儿. Can you distinguish the following three characters? 元　远　玩

我明天要去法國, 要買一些法國錢.	我明天要去法国, 要买一些法国钱.
現在不能買法國錢, 得買歐元.	现在不能买法国钱, 得买欧元.

Currencies:

美元	欧元／歐元	加拿大元	日元

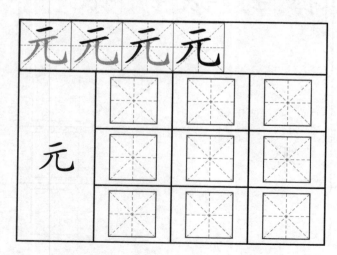

買/买 (mǎi)

mǎi	Ancient Form	Later Form	Modern Traditional Form	Modern Simplified Form
buy			買	买
mǎi dōngxi			買東西	买东西

The bottom component of 貴/贵 (*guì*, 'honorable') is the radical for 'cowry shell' 貝/贝 (*bèi*) (used as 'money' in ancient times). So it makes nice sense for 買/买 (*mǎi*, 'to buy') to have the same radical, at least in the traditional version—but what's happened to the simplified form? The key to meaning has disappeared! In its place is *tóu* 头/頭, (裡頭的頭). Sometimes I can't figure out the simplification process. Be careful, the next character up is 賣/卖 (*mài*, 'sell'), a look-alike.

你今天下午想到哪兒去？ 　—我想出去买东西. 買甚麼東西？ 　—我甚麼都想買, 可是不能, 錢不夠.	你今天下午想到哪儿去？ 　—我想出去買東西. 买什么东西？ 　—我什么都想买, 可是不能, 钱不够.

買賣/买卖 buy + sell = 'business; trade'	買東西/买东西 buy + things/stuff = 'shop'

Modern Traditional Form	Modern Simplified Form
買 買 買 買 買 買 買 買 買 買 買 買 買	买 买 买 买 买 买 买

賣／卖 (*mài*)

mài	Ancient Form	Modern Traditional Form	Modern Simplified Form
sell	𧶠	賣	卖
zuò mǎimài		做買賣	做买卖

Assuming you just learned about 買／买 (*mǎi*, 'buy'), here's that look-alike we promised you. Put 十 (*shí*, 'ten') on top of 買／买 and you get 賣／卖 (*mài*, 'sell'), which has the same radical as 買 (*mǎi*) in its traditional form—貝／贝—and the same 'radical' surgery in its simplified form. Keep *mǎi* and *mài* separate just as you do 'buy' and 'sell' in English.

你將來想做甚麼？ 　　—我想做買賣，做買賣很有意思。 做買賣也可以賺很多錢。	你将来想做什么？ 　　—我想做买卖，做买卖很有意思。 做买卖也可以赚很多钱。

買賣／买卖 buy + sell = 'business; trade'	買國／买国 sell + country = 'betray one's country'

Modern Traditional Form	Modern Simplified Form

貴/贵 (*guì*)

guì	Ancient Form	Modern Traditional Form	Modern Simplified Form
expensive; costly; honorable	𧵑	貴	贵
Guìxìng?		貴姓?	贵姓?

The bottom component of 貴/贵 (*guì*) is 貝/贝 (*bèi*, 'cowry shell')—'money' in our world. The top part, 臾 (*guì* [altered]), is a 'basket,' so we've got a 'basket of money,' something very costly, very expensive, something that could bring honor and status to someone. You will see the radical 貝/贝 as part of two 'look-alikes' and 'sound-alikes': 買/买 (*mǎi*, 'buy') and 賣/卖 (*mài*, 'sell'), both of which can involve expense.

兩百塊錢太貴了! 能不能便宜一點兒? 　—不貴不貴! 東西好, 東西好! 你賣得太貴了, 我不買了, 我走了.	两百块钱太贵了! 能不能便宜一点儿. 　—不贵不贵! 东西好, 东西好! 你卖得太贵了, 我不买了, 我走了.

貴姓/贵姓? honorable + surname = 'Your name, please?'	高貴/高贵 high + expensive/honorable = 'noble'

Modern Traditional Form	Modern Simplified Form

便 (*pián*)

pián	Ancient Form	Modern Form
(cheap; inexpensive)	便	便
piányi		便宜

便 (*pián*) is a very flexible character in that it has, like some Chinese characters, two pronunciations, each rendering different meanings, yet both, in a sense, related to the radical 亻(*rén*, 'person'; the full form is 人). Here's the scoop: 便 (*pián*) joins with 宜 (*yí*) and we get 便宜 (*piányi*, 'cheap'), relevant for this unit; however, the same character, when pronounced *biàn*, joins with 方 (*fāng*) to give us 方便 (*fāngbiàn*, 'convenient'). Another 'two-for-one'! But that's not all. 更 (*gèng*), the right side of 便, means 'even more.' Remember this: 你很高, 可是他更高 ('You're tall, but he's even taller').

因為家裡錢不夠, 所以我太太只能買便宜的東西, 不能買貴的.	因为家里钱不够, 所以我太太只能买便宜的东西, 不能买贵的.

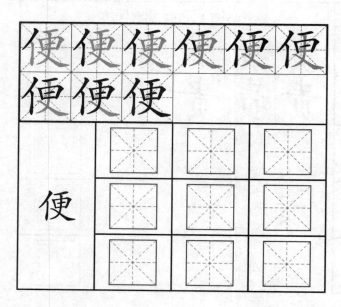

宜 (yí)

yí	Ancient Form	Later Form	Modern Form
(cheap)	![ancient form]	![later form]	宜
piányi			便宜

Some characters respond more easily to 'clue-ing' than others. 宜 (*yí*) is one of those others. The ancient form is like a sketch of two pieces of sacrificial meat on two altars. That is hardly a suitable clue for 'cheap.' Maybe the gods thought two pieces just too cheap. Keep in mind that the *yí* in *piányi* 便宜 is neutral tone. Also note the 'roof' radical in the modern form, which you have seen before in 家 (*jiā*, 'home').

你去買東西, 不要買太便宜的, 也不要買太貴的.	你去买东西, 不要买太便宜的, 也不要买太贵的.

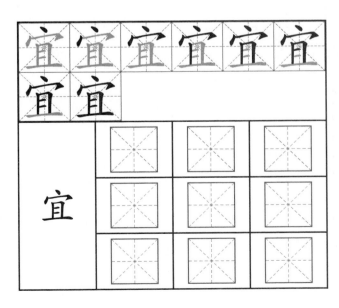

比 (bǐ)

bǐ	Ancient Form	Later Form	Modern Form
compare with/to; than	屮屮	𠤐	比
Wǒ bǐ tā gāo.			我比她高.

比 (bǐ) is a sketch of two persons side by side, perhaps comparing each other. The two sides are nearly identical, compared with one another. But be careful, for when you actually do compare them, they are not quite the same. When you write the character, compare each side carefully; don't forget the upward sweep on the left and the 'flourish' on the right.

怎麼黑的比白的貴點兒? 　—黑的, 東西好, 白的不能比, 所以貴點 　兒. 你賣得比別的地方貴點兒, 我不買.	怎么黑的比白的贵点儿? 　—黑的, 东西好, 白的不能比, 所以贵点 　儿. 你卖得比别的地方贵点儿, 我不买.

不能比 not + able + compare = 　'incomparable'	比薩 / 比萨 Bǐsà = 'pizza; Pisa (Italy)' 盧比 / 卢比 *lúbǐ* = 'rupee' (*monetary unit of India*)

比 比 比 比

比

跟 (gēn)

gēn	Ancient Form	Modern Form
(together) with; and (*joins nouns, not clauses*)	跟	跟
Wǒ gén nǐ qù.		我跟你去.

The radical on the left (the full form, 足, is altered slightly when a radical) means 'foot,' or, by extension, 'to follow' (after someone) and be together with him or her. The right part, the phonetic, 艮 (*gěn/en*), is a particularly rich phonetic for us because it provides an excellent sound clue for 很 (*hěn*, 'very'), though a less reliable one for 銀/银 (*yín*, 'silver'). 跟 and 和 (*hé*) are roughly parallel, both meaning 'and.'

跟, 和, 兩個字的意思差不多.	跟, 和, 两个字的意思差不多.
我和你一起去買, 好不好?	我和你一起去买, 好不好?
我的書跟你的一樣貴.	我的书跟你的一样贵.

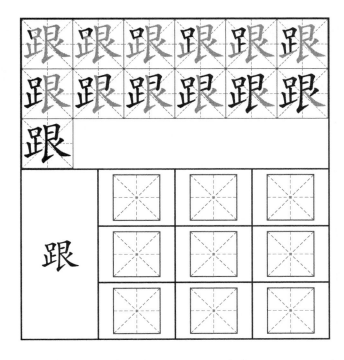

少 (shǎo)

shǎo	Ancient Form	Later Form	Modern Simplified Form
less	小	少	少
duōshǎo			多少

You already know the character *xiǎo* 小 'small.' Well, add a downward slash to the left and 小 becomes *shǎo* 少. The two are so close that you need to be careful to distinguish them. The ancient form of 少 is a sketch of four grains of sand, and the ancient form of 小 is a sketch of three grains. 小 therefore, then and now, means 'small in size,' while 少 means 'small in number.' Also note that sometimes you will see the first stroke of this character (the one in the middle) printed without the upward 'hook.' English has many different font forms; so does Chinese.

老闆 (*lǎobǎn*), 這個多少錢?	老板 (*lǎobǎn*), 这个多少钱?
這個要多少美金?	这个要多少美金?
我吃的太多了, 你吃的太少了.	我吃的太多了, 你吃的太少了.
一百塊錢太少了, 我不賣。	一百块钱太少了, 我不卖。

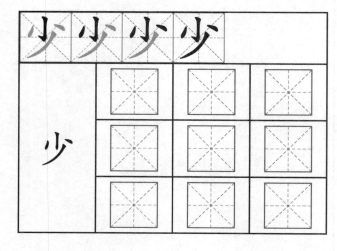

太 (tài)

tài	Ancient Form	Modern Form
too; extremely; overly	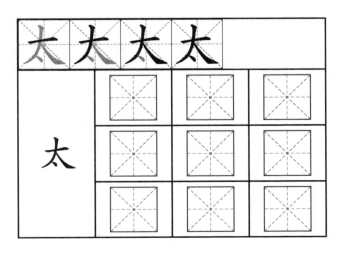	太
Tài guì le!		太貴了 / 太贵了!

太 (*tài*) is formed by adding a stroke to the character 大 (*dà*, 'big; great'). Adding an additional stroke to 'great' makes 'great' extremely 'great.' In speech, 太 often attracts 了 (*le*), frequently with negative implications, but sometimes with the positive in mind as well. In the following phrases, can you distinguish the positive from the negative?

太小了	太高了	太累了	太貴了 / 太贵了	太多了	太大了
太黑了	太好了	太有意思了	太没有意思了	太忙了	太冷了

太太 extremely + grand = 'Mrs.; wife'	王太太 = 'Mrs. Wang'
太平 great + peace = 'peace (on earth)'	太极拳 grand + ultimate + fist = *tàijíquán*, 'Taichi, Chinese exercise/shadow boxing'

太 太 大 太

太

能 (néng)

néng	Ancient Form	Modern Form
able to; can	𤱀	能
nénggòu		能夠 / 能够

In ancient times the character 能 (néng) originally meant 'bear.' See the claws on the right? Later the character was 'borrowed' in the loan process to mean 'able to; can' [if circumstances permit]). The meaning of 'bear' is now represented by a new character, 熊 (xióng), with four dots added at the bottom. The relevant word for this unit is 能夠 / 能够 (nénggòu, 'able to; capable of').

你明天能不能跟我去買東西？ 　—不能去, 我有點兒事。 後天也不能去嗎？ 　—不, 後天能去, 沒事。	你明天能不能跟我去买东西？ 　—不能去, 我有点儿事. 后天也不能去吗？ 　—不, 后天能去, 没事.

能夠 / 能够 able + enough = 'able to'	可能 may + able = 'possibly, maybe; possible'
能人 capability + person = 'able person'	才能 talent + capability = 'talent'

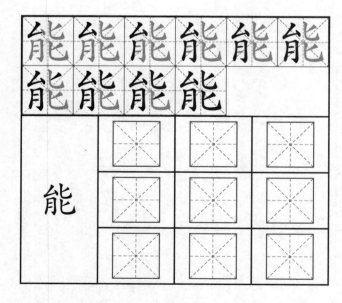

　Copyright © 2012 by Yale University and China International Publishing Group

夠/够 (gòu)

gòu	Ancient Form	Modern Traditional Form	Modern Simplified Form
enough	夠	夠	够
Gòu le!		夠了!	够了!

Isn't it great to run into a character that has a component already familiar to you? You know the right part. It's 多 (*duō*, 'many'), two 'moons,' one on top of another. Two moons are quite enough, thank you. Now 夠/够 is my kind of character because the traditional form and the simplified form are simply reverse forms of one another, and two forms of the same character are quite enough for me. 句 (*gōu*) on the left is the phonetic component.

三百塊錢夠不夠? —可能不夠, 多給點兒. 三百塊不夠, 我就不買. —你不要買, 那我就不賣.	三百块钱够不够? —可能不够, 多给点儿. 三百块不够, 我就不买. —你不要买, 那, 我就不卖.

Modern Traditional Form	Modern Simplified Form
夠 夠 夠 夠 夠 夠 夠 夠 夠 夠 夠 夠	够 够 够 够 够 够 够 够 够 够 够 够

給/给 (gěi)

gěi	Ancient Form	Modern Traditional Form	Modern Simplified Form
to give; for (the benefit of)	給	給	给
Wo gěi qián.		我給錢.	我给钱.

給/给 (gěi) is a typical two-component, picto-phonetic character. 糸 / 纟 on the left is the signific component, relating the character to 'silk.' 合 on the right means 'joined,' so 'joined threads of silk.' Memory aid? 'Silk' is an important part of Chinese culture, and giving a gift of silk to someone is paying them a great compliment. So remember that the giving of 'silk' (糸 / 纟) will give an opportunity to tightly join (合) a friendship.

媽媽, 給我買一塊糖!	妈妈, 给我买一块糖!
你給她買一塊糖吃, 好不好?	你给她买一块糖吃, 好不好?
我沒有錢. 你給錢, 好不好?	我没有钱. 你给钱, 好不好?

Modern Traditional Form	Modern Simplified Form
給 給 給 給 給 給 給 給 給 給 給 給 給	给 给 给 给 给 给 给 给 给

Unit 10

The sentences below are inspired by the contents of Unit 10 and contain all the new characters required for writing as well as others. Read and reread until fluent, covering the English as you read. Then cover the English and try to reproduce the Chinese equivalents orally. Do this exercise before beginning to practice writing.

遠東百貨商店賣的東西便宜不便宜? 远东百货商店卖的东西便宜不便宜?	Are the things sold at the Far East Department Store cheap or not?
你家在北邊兒還是在南邊兒? 你家在北边儿还是在南边儿?	Is your home in the north or in the south?
我很想去看看天安門廣場. 離這兒遠嗎? 我很想去看看天安门广场. 离这儿远吗?	I'd like to go and have a look at Tian'anmen Square. Is it far from here?
明年你跟我到中國去, 好不好? 明年你跟我到中国去, 好不好?	Next year, let's you and I go to China, okay?
我小弟弟很想學開車. 我小弟弟很想学开车.	My little brother would like to learn to drive.
你的東西都在上面, 不在下面. 你的東西都在上面, 不在下面	Your things are on top, not on the bottom.
路太遠, 你得開車去. 路太远, 你得开车去.	It's too far; you will have to drive.
學生中心在那邊兒嗎? 学生中心在那边儿吗?	Is the student center over there?
近來買日用品越來越貴. 近来买日用品越来越贵	Recently (jìnlái), buying everyday things is getting more and more expensive.

Matching Exercise

Match the radical, basic meaning, and character.

食 / 饣	太	sleep
忄	意	home; family
王	睡	too; excessively
糸 / 纟	飯 / 饭	(open) field
心	家	red
土	紅 / 红	goods; articles
目	忙	road
宀	玩	hundred(s)
大	場 / 场	idea
足	洗	wash; clean
貝 / 贝	百	play; amuse oneself
白	邊 / 边	busy
氵	貨 / 货	food; rice
辵 / 辶	路	side (of something)

用 (yòng)

yòng	Ancient Form	Later Form	Modern Form
to use, utilize; with (the aid of)	用	用	用
rìyòngpǐn			日用品

Let's remember that the fewer the writing strokes in a character, the more difficult the formulation of a clue. 用 (*yòng*) is an example. Some claim that the original meaning of 用 is 'barrel.' Do you see a barrel in 用? Share some ideas for other memory aids with your classmates. Use your imagination. Take a look at some 用 look-alikes. Distinguish 用, 周, 网, and 同.

哪個地方賣日用品? —前面有一個. 走十分鐘就到了.	哪个地方卖日用品? —前面有一个. 走十分钟就到了.

用心 use + heart = 'with concentrated attention; diligently'	用筷子吃飯 / 用筷子吃饭 'eat with chopsticks' (*kuàizi*)
信用卡 trust + use + card = 'credit card'	日用品 daily + use + article = 'commodity'

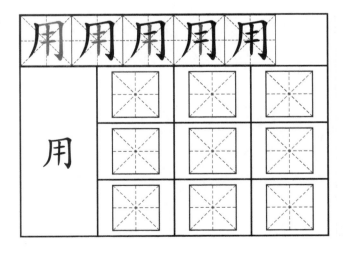

心 (*xīn*)

xīn	Ancient Form	Later Form	Modern Form
heart			心
zhōngxīn			中心

心 (*xīn*) is a pictograph of the human heart, and a pretty good picture at that. It is a character associated not only with 'heart' but also with heartfelt feelings, the mind, the core of things, the center, the middle of things. Our relevant compound is 購物中心/购物中心 (*gòuwù zhōngxīn*, 'shopping center'). 心 is a very important radical, as we have seen before in the following: 您, 想, 念, 意, 思, 急, 怎. Can you recall all of them? Usually 心 appears as 忄 when it is a character component, as in 忙 (*máng*, 'busy').

Useful compounds:

點心 / 点心	小心	用心	心事	心上人
diǎnxīn	*xiǎoxīn*	*yòngxīn*	*xīnshì*	*xīnshàngrén*
dessert; snack	be careful	be diligent	private worries	sweetheart

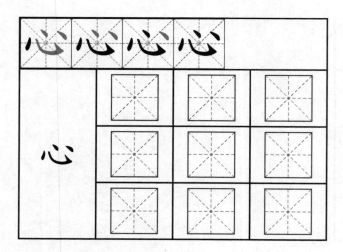

kāi	Ancient Form	Modern Traditional Form	Modern Simplified Form
to open; to start; to drive	閂	開	开
kāi chē		開車	开车

開/开 (*kāi*) is a great character. It really talks to us. There's the 'door' (we've seen 'door' before in 們 and 問), and there's the opening right there in the middle, 开. The character has many applications, everything from opening a door, to turning on a light, to driving a car, to boiling water—all actions involving opening or starting something. I love one of the early forms; you can actually see hands opening the door! As it happened, the simplification process eliminated the 'door' but left the 'opening.'

我每天走路回家, 你呢? 　　—我每天跟我姐姐回家, 她開車, 很快就 　　　到了.	我每天走路回家, 你呢? 　　—我每天跟我姐姐回家, 她开车, 很快就 　　　到了.

開車 / 开车 to start + vehicle = 'to drive'	開心 / 开心 to open + heart = 'happy; joyful'
開口 / 开口 to open + mouth = 'speak'	開水 / 开水 open + water = 'boiled water'

Modern Traditional Form	Modern Simplified Form
開 開 開 開 開 開 開 開 開 開 開 開 開	开 开 开 开 开

車／车 (*chē*)

chē	Ancient Form	Later Form	Modern Traditional Form	Modern Simplified Form
vehicle; cart; car	車	車	車	车
kāi chē			開車	开车

車／车 (*chē*) is a sketch of a wheeled chariot viewed from above, easily seen in the ancient form but less visible in the modern versions, especially the simplified form. The character is richly employed in Chinese to express all sorts of vehicles from 'trains' (火車／火车) to 'bicycles' (自行車／自行车). Here's a sampling, some more useful in our modern world than others:

馬車 马车 *mǎchē* cart	汽車 汽车 *qìchē* car	開車 开车 *kāi chē* to drive	貨車 货车 *huòchē* truck	火車 火车 *huǒchē* train	公車 公车 *gōngchē* public bus	牛車 牛车 *niúchē* ox-cart

Here's an interesting character, with three *chē*: 轟／轰 (*hōng*), meaning 'the sound of many carts' > 'hubbub; sensation.' It is not frequently used in modern Chinese, but it is a fun character nonetheless.

Modern Traditional Form	Modern Simplified Form
車 車 車 車 車 車 車 　車	车 车 车 车 　车

到 (dào)

dào	Ancient Form	Modern Form
arrive, reach; to (a place); *(indicates completion of an action)*	业	到
dào Rìběn qù		到日本去

到 (*dào*) is a typical side-by-side, two-component character, with a nice phonetic, 刀 (*dāo*, 'knife'). 刀 is usually is written as 刂 when a component. 至 (*zhì*) on the left means 'to arrive' and is the signific/meaning indicator. Distinguish 别 (*bié*) from 到.

走這條路能到北京大學嗎? 　—不. 你得往南走才行. 好, 多謝, 多謝.	走这条路能到北京大学吗? 　—不. 你得往南走才行. 好, 多谢, 多谢.

拿到 = 'get; attain'	一直到 = 'until, up to' (in time or space)
回到 = 'return to'	等到 = 'wait until'

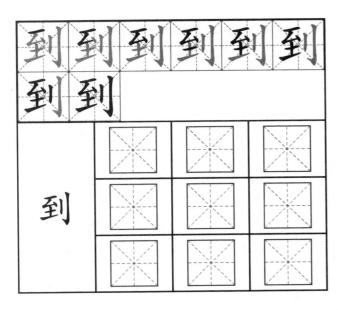

百 (bǎi)

bǎi	Ancient Form	Later Form	Modern Form
hundred	⊖	百	百
yìbǎi, liǎngbǎi, sānbǎi…			一百, 兩(两)百, 三百

Let's break 百 (bǎi) into two parts: top 一 and bottom 白 (bái, 'white'), the phonetic, and we wind up with yìbǎi ('one hundred'). So 'one plus white' equals 'one hundred.' Make sense? Probably not in other worlds, but in our Chinese 'world' it sort of does. Hope it makes one hundred percent sense to you.

今天去遠東百貨商店買東西, 好嗎? —那個百貨商店東西太貴了, 我不去.	今天去远东百货商店买东西, 好吗? —那个百货商店东西太贵了, 我不去.

老百姓 old + hundred + surnames = 'the common people'	百貨商店 / 百货商店 hundreds + goods + business + store = 'shopping center'

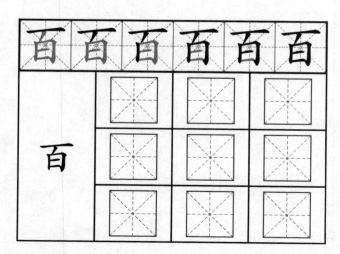

貨/货 (huò)

huò	Ancient Form	Modern Traditional Form	Modern Simplified Form
commodities, goods, products	貨	貨	货
bǎihuòshāngdiàn		百貨商店	百货商店

貨/货 (huò) is the next character up. The top part is 化 (huà), the phonetic component, which is not much help. 貨/货 means 'commodities, goods, or products'; thus, it is about selling and buying with money. The bottom part of 貨/货 is the radical 貝/贝 ('cowrie shell')—used for currency in ancient times, meaning 'money,' money to buy goods and products. Review and distinguish 貨/货, 貴/贵, 買/买, and 賣/卖.

"一分錢一分貨." 老師, 我說的對不對? 　　—不太對, 應該是 "一分價錢 (jiàqián, prices) 一分貨."	"一分钱一分货." 老师, 我说的对不对? 　　—不太对, 应该是 "一分价钱 (jiàqián, prices) 一分货."

貨車／货车 goods + vehicle = 'truck'	日用百貨／日用百货 day + use + hundred + goods = 'daily use goods/commodities'

Modern Traditional Form	Modern Simplified Form
貨 貨 貨 貨 貨 貨 貨 貨 貨 貨 貨 貨	货 货 货 货 货 货 货 货 货

商 (shāng)

shāng	Ancient Form	Later Form	Modern Form
trade; business	羊	啇	商
shāngdiàn			商店

The original meaning of 商 (shāng) was 'to discuss; consult.' Perhaps that's why we see a 口 (kǒu, 'mouth') within it. Well, how to we get to 'commerce; trade; business'? A good businessman is a good talker. Hold on—is that a 'hat' on top? Another link?

老師, 商字是甚麼意思? 　—商字是買賣的意思.	老师, 商字是什么意思? 　—商字是买卖的意思.

商場 / 商场 business + field = 'shopping center'	百貨商店 / 百货商店 hundred + goods + business + store = 'department store'
商人 business + person = 'businessperson; tradesperson'	商店 commerce + store = 'store; shop'

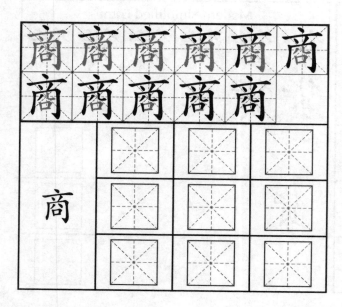

場/场 (*chǎng*)

chǎng	Ancient Form	Later Form	Modern Traditional Form	Modern Simplified Form
open place; site	畾	場	場	场
shāngchǎng			商場	商场

The original meaning of 場/场 (*chǎng*) is 'an open place where people gather to worship.' The left side is a radical we've seen before, 土 (*tǔ*, 'earth'), (also seen in 地, 在, 坐, 址). 場/场 is now used for any open place, everything from a shopping plaza, a farm, an airport, a market, a theater, and even a battlefield, all requiring a 'site' or 'open space' of some sort, therefore the left-side 土 radical. The right part, 易 (*yáng*), is the 'near' phonetic, which in ancient times meant 'the sun's rays piercing through the clouds,' in an open field, perhaps.

前面是不是天安門廣場? 　—對! 你一直往前走就到了.	前面是不是天安门广场? 　—对! 你一直往前走就到了.

商場/商场 trade + site = 'shopping center'	天安門廣場/天安门广场 (*Tiānānmén guǎngchǎng*) = 'Tian'anmen Square'

Modern Traditional Form	Modern Simplified Form
場 場 場 場 場 場 場 場 場 場 場 場 場	场 场 场 场 场 场 场

店 (diàn)

diàn	Ancient Form	Modern Form
shop, store; inn/hotel (in names of hotels)	坫	店
shāngdiàn		商店

店 (*diàn*, 'store; shop') has 广 ('*shed*'—perhaps where the store is?) as its radical, and a pretty reliable phonetic, 占, one you've seen before. Remember 占 in 一點/一点 (*yīdiǎn*)? It has the same phonetic reminder. Let's link the two sounds. A purist will maintain that 占 is actually pronounced *zhàn*, and that's correct. But I'll stick with *diàn*. Clues are the important factor to me.

遠東百貨商店跟日月商店東西一樣嗎?	远东百货商店跟日月商店东西一样吗?
東西差不多, 可是價錢不一樣. 日月商店貴一點兒. (價錢 [*jiàqian*] = 'prices')	东西差不多, 可是价钱不一样. 日月商店贵一点儿. (价钱 [*jiàqian*] = 'prices')

商店 business + shop = 'shopping center'	飯店 / 饭店 = 'hotel'
客店 guest + store = 'hotel'	酒店 (*jiǔdiàn*) = 'bar; tavern'
北京飯店 / 北京饭店 = 'Beijing Hotel'	書店 / 书店 = 'bookstore'

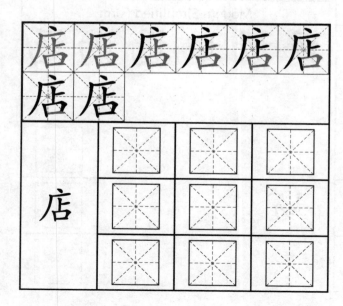

lù	Ancient Form	Modern Form
road; (*used in measuring distance*)		路
yī lǐ lù		一里路

路 (*lù*) is a much used character, often appearing in words relating to roads or measurement of distance. Appropriately, the left side is 足 ('foot'), which is a radical we've seen before, in 跟 (*gēn*, 'to follow, accompany'). The right part is a character in itself, 各 (*gè*), meaning 'each.' So, 'each foot must follow its own path.' Useful 路 compounds:

路上	馬路 / 马路	路口	走路	問路 / 问路	近路
on the road / way	street, avenue	intersection	walk	ask directions	shortcut

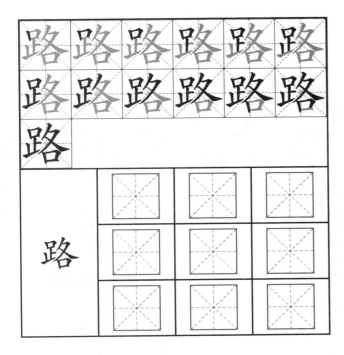

zuǒ	Ancient Form	Later Form	Modern Simplified Form
left (side)			左
zuǒbiānr			左邊兒 / 左边儿

yòu	Ancient Form	Later Form	Modern Simplified Form
right (side)			右
yòubiānr			右邊兒 / 右边儿

Two for one on this page! The key to 左 (*zuǒ*, 'left') is 右 (*yòu*, 'right'), and vice versa. These two characters—左 and 右—are among the most confused by students of Chinese. Just as you, as a youngster, had to get straight which hand was the left and which the right, so, too, with these two. Well, 'left' has 工 (*gōng*, 'work')—the left-handed worker? 'Right' has 口 (*kǒu*, 'mouth'): if it's 口 it must be 右—right! Hope this helps, and our 'two for one' approach results in your knowing your left from your right!

nán	Ancient Form	Later Form	Modern Simplified Form
south	首	𦰩	南
nánbiānr			南邊兒 / 南边儿

南 (*nán*) is a 'loan' character whose original meaning, 'bell,' is very evident, especially in the later form. 南 was 'loaned' out to provide a character for the meaning 'south,' and it is now used in directional words, such as 西南, 東南/东南, 南邊/南边; and also in names of places in the south. Here are a few:

河南 'south of the (Yellow) river' > *Hénán* Province
湖南 'south of the (Dong Ting) lake' > *Húnán* Province
雲南 / 云南 'south of the clouds' > *Yúnnán* Province
南京 'the southern capital' > *Nánjīng*
南美(洲) 'South America'

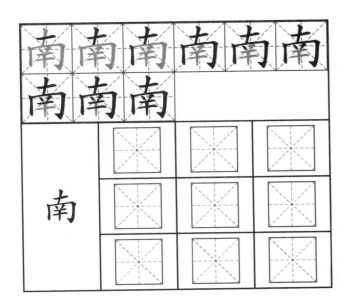

北 (běi)

běi	Ancient Form	Later Form	Modern Form
north; northern	北	北	北
běibiānr			北邊兒／北边儿

北 (běi) 'talks' to me and says: 'two opposing forces, one north and one south, at opposite poles.' It is very different from 比 (bǐ)—still two forces, but rather alike when compared. 北 vs. 比, 比 vs. 北. Keep both in mind when learning either. The original meaning of 北 was 'back of one's body'—that meaning is now represented by 背 (bèi). Both are likely phonetic loans, but that doesn't help us much. What helps is reminding ourselves of their similiarities and differences.

比字跟北字很像可是不一樣. 意思也不一樣.	比字跟北字很像可是不一样. 意思也不一样.

('bǐ and běi resemble [xiàng] one another but are different.')

西北 west + north = 'northwest'	東北／东北 east + north = 'northeast'
北京 north + capital = 'Beijing'	北邊兒／北边儿 north + side = 'north'

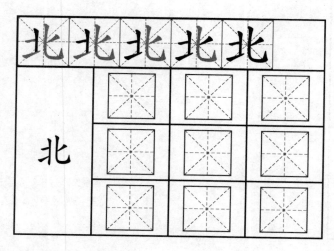

面 (miàn)

miàn	Ancient Form	Later Form	Modern Form
face; side; surface; aspect			面
shàngmian			上面

I don't see a 'face' in 面 (miàn). I see a building with a ladder going up, maybe with a fire-fighter going up to face the danger. Others see 目 (*mù*, 'eye') inside—maybe that helps.

Can you figure out the meanings of the following words?

上面	裡面 / 里面	前面	東面 / 东面	南面
下面	外面	后面	西面	北面

面子 face + *zi* = 'the concept of "face" in Chinese society'	水面 water + face/surface = 'surface of the water'
见面 see + face = 'meet' (someone)	地面 land + surface = 'the earth's surface'

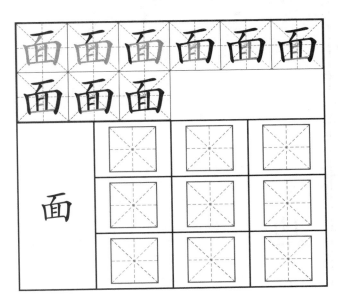

biān	Ancient Form	Modern Traditional Form	Modern Simplified Form
side; edge; border		邊	边
shàngbiānr		上邊兒	上边儿

The original meaning of 邊/边 (*biān*) is 'the edge of a cliff.' 辵/辶 is the radical, indicating the character is related to 'walking.' We've seen this radical before. Recall 過/过, 道, 近, 這/这, 週/周, and 遠/远. Take a careful look at 邊. It's one of the most complicated characters we've seen, nearly 20 strokes. The simplified form combines the radical with 力 (*lì*, 'power, strength'). (We have encountered 力 before in 男.) 邊/边 often takes the 'r' ending, becoming *biānr*, and combines with many, many words indicating location. Here are just a few. How many do you know?

這邊	那邊	上邊	下邊	左邊	右邊	裡邊	外邊	前邊
外邊	東邊	西邊	南邊	北邊	兩邊	四邊	路邊	海邊

这边	那边	上边	下边	左边	右边	里边	外边	前边
外边	东边	西边	南边	北边	两边	四边	路边	海边

Modern Traditional Form	Modern Simplified Form
邊	边

Copyright © 2012 by Yale University and China International Publishing Group

近 (jìn)

jìn	Ancient Form	Modern Form
near; close	訢	近
lí zhèr hěn jìn		離這兒很近 / 离这儿很近

The character 近 (jìn) epitomizes the typical formation of radical plus phonetic. It doesn't get any better than this. There's the radical 辶 ('going; movement; walking') on the left (recall 遠/远 [yuǎn]), reminding us that we're getting closer and closer. And there's the phonetic 斤 (jīn), quite reliable here, except for the tone. 斤 is a useful character in itself, as it is a common unit of weight used in China, equal to about 1⅓ pounds.

那個地方不近, 很遠, 可是有一個近路. 走近路很方便.	那个地方不近, 很远, 可是有一个近路. 走近路很方便.
遠近 / 远近 far + near = 'distance'	近來 / 近来 close + come = 'recently'
近路 close + road = 'shortcut'	近年 close + years = 'recent years'

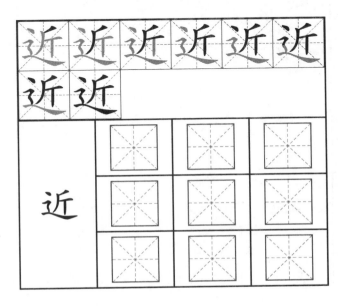

yuǎn	Ancient Form	Later Form	Modern Traditional Form	Modern Simplified Form
far; remote			遠	远
tài yuǎn le			太遠了	太远了

Sometimes, thankfully, the simplification process results in a character that is easier to remember. 遠/远 (*yuǎn*, 'far') is an excellent example. After all, if you have already learned 元 (*yuán*, 'dollar'), just add the 辵/辶 ('walking' radical) to reach far. I can't offer much for the traditional form, except to say that the phonetic is 袁 (*yuán*). Here's a reminder about some look-alikes: 元, 远, 玩, and 完. Can you distinguish them? Can you use each in a sentence?

離這兒不遠有一家商店, 東西又好又便宜. 你應該去看看.	离这儿不远有一家商店, 东西又好又便宜. 你应该去看看.

Modern Traditional Form	Modern Simplified Form
遠 遠 遠 遠 遠 遠 遠 遠 遠 遠 遠 遠 遠 遠	远 远 远 远 远 远 远

遠

远

離/离 (lí)

lí	Ancient Form	Modern Traditional Form	Modern Simplified Form
from, away from, distance from	离	離	离
lí zhèr hěn yuǎn		離這兒很遠	离这儿很远

My clue for 離/离 (lí) is the radical on the right, 隹 ('bird'), which is new to us. I've always thought the left side looked like a nest and the bird was flying away from it. Then, when I learned the simplified character, I found that the bird had indeed gone from the nest—the radical had disappeared! But the association was enough and has served me well. I hope it does for you as well.

哪兒有賣書的地方? —離這兒不到一里路, 有一個書店.	哪儿有卖书的地方? —离这儿不到一里路, 有一个书店.

離開 / 离开 leave + open = 'depart from'	離不開 / 离不开 leave + not + open = 'cannot be separated from; cannot do without'

Modern Traditional Form	Modern Simplified Form
離 離 離 離 離 離 離 離 離 離 離 離 離 離 離 離 離 離 離	离 离 离 离 离 离 离 离 离 离

離

离

Index I: Characters Arranged by Pinyin

lǐ	裡/里	123
liǎng	兩/两	119
liù	六	8
lù	路	225

M

ma	嗎/吗	20
mā	媽/妈	111
mài	賣/卖	202
mǎi	買/买	201
máng	忙	169
me	麼/么	37
méi	沒	100
mèi	妹	113
měi	美	90
měi	每	191
men	們/们	34
mén	門/门	185
miàn	面	229
míng	名	38
mò	末	176
mù	木	12
mǔ	母	109

N

nà/néi	那	48
nǎ/něi	哪	49
nán	男	117
nán	南	227
néng	能	210
nǐ	你	23
nián	年	54
niàn	念	145
nín	您	42
nǚ	女	118

P

pián	便	204

Q

qǐ	起	30
qī	期	78
qī	七	8
qián	錢/钱	134
qián	前	187
qīn	親/亲	110
qǐng	請/请	21
qù	去	101

R

rè	熱/热	166
rén	人	13
rì	日	56

S

sān	三	7
shān	山	14
shàng	上	65
shāng	商	222
shǎo	少	208
shén	甚/什	36
shēng	生	58
shí	時/时	79
shí	十	9
shì	是	24
shì	事	83
shì	視/视	181
shǒu	手	190
shuì	睡	177
shuǐ	水	15
shuō	說/说	95
sì	四	7
sī	思	147

suì	歲/岁	71

T

tā	他	33
tā	她	127
tài	太	209
tiān	天	68

W

wán	玩	183
wǎn	晚	70
wǎng	網/网	184
wèi	位	46
wèi	為/为	136
wén	文	92
wǒ	我	25
wǔ	午	71
wǔ	五	8

X

xǐ	喜	93
xǐ	洗	189
xī	西	158
xià	下	66
xiàn	現/现	72
xiǎng	想	129
xiǎo	小	44
xiè	謝/谢	32
xīn	心	216
xìng	姓	31
xìng	興/兴	163
xīng	星	77
xiōng	兄	114

Y

yàng	樣/样	161
yào	要	130

yě	也	126	yuán	元	200	zhǐ	址	61
yí	宜	205	yuǎn	遠/远	232	zhī	知	138
yì	意	147	yuè	月	55	zhōng	中	87
yǐ	以	186				zhōu	週/周	175
yī	一	7	**Z**			zhuàn	賺/赚	133
yín	銀/银	199	zài	再	26	zì	字	39
yīn	因	135	zài	在	73	zǒu	走	154
yǐng	影	182	zǎo	早	69	zuǒ	左	226
yīng	英	91	zěn	怎	160	zuò	做	141
yòng	用	215	zháo	著/着	164	zuò	坐	153
yǒu	有	82	zhè/zhèi	這/这	47			
yóu	右	226	zhě	者	144			

Index II: Characters Arranged by Number of Strokes

1

一	yī	7

2

八	bā	9
儿	ér	50
二	èr	7
几	jǐ	51
九	jiǔ	9
了	le	53
七	qī	8
人	rén	13
十	shí	9

3

才	cái	122
大	dà	43
个	gè	120
口	kǒu	11
么	me	37
门	mén	185
女	nǚ	118
三	sān	7
山	shān	14
上	shàng	65
下	xià	66
小	xiǎo	44
也	yě	126

4

比	bǐ	206
不	bù	29
车	chē	218
分	fēn	75
父	fù	107

火	huǒ	10
见	jiàn	27
今	jīn	67
开	kāi	217
六	liù	8
木	mù	12
日	rì	56
少	shǎo	208
什	shén	36
手	shǒu	190
水	shuǐ	15
太	tài	209
天	tiān	68
为	wèi	136
文	wén	92
五	wǔ	8
午	wǔ	71
心	xīn	216
元	yuán	200
月	yuè	55
中	zhōng	87

5

白	bái	197
半	bàn	74
北	běi	228
边	biān	230
出	chū	103
电	diàn	180
东	dōng	157
对	duì	28
号	hào	52
叫	jiào	35
们	men	34
末	mò	176

母	mǔ	109
去	qù	101
生	shēng	58
四	sì	7
他	tā	32
兄	xiōng	114
以	yǐ	186
用	yòng	215
左	yòu	226
右	zuǒ	226

6

百	bǎi	220
场	chǎng	223
吃	chī	156
当	dāng	140
地	dì	60
多	duō	45
过	guò	102
好	hǎo	19
红	hóng	196
后	hòu	188
欢	huān	94
回	huí	155
会	huì	97
级	jí	146
吗	ma	20
妈	mā	111
买	mǎi	201
忙	máng	169
名	míng	38
那	nà	48
年	nián	54
岁	suì	57
她	tā	127

网	wǎng	184
西	xī	158
兴	xìng	164
因	yīn	135
有	yǒu	82
再	zài	26
在	zài	73
早	zǎo	69
字	zì	39

7

吧	ba	159
别	bié	142
車	chē	218
弟	dì	116
饭	fàn	171
还	hái	128
见	jiàn	27
来	lái	132
冷	lěng	167
里	lǐ	123
两	liǎng	119
没	méi	100
每	měi	191
男	nán	117
你	nǐ	23
时	shí	79
位	wèi	46
我	wǒ	25
远	yòng	232
这	zhè	47
址	zhǐ	61
走	zǒu	154
坐	zuò	153

8

| 爸 | bà | 108 |

饱	bǎo	172
到	dào	219
的	de	59
店	diàn	224
東	dōng	157
兒	ér	50
国	guó	88
和	hé	121
话	huà	96
货	huò	221
或	huò	143
姐	jiě	112
近	jìn	231
金	jīn	198
來	lái	132
两	liǎng	119
卖	mài	202
妹	mèi	113
門	mén	185
念	niàn	145
事	shì	83
视	shì	181
玩	wán	183
现	xiàn	72
姓	xìng	31
宜	yí	205
英	yīng	91
者	zhě	144
知	zhī	138
周	zhōu	175

9

帮	bāng	137
点	diǎn	76
给	gěi	212
贵	guì	203
红	hóng	196

後	hòu	188
急	jí	165
将	jiāng	131
觉	jiào/jué	178
看	kàn	179
美	měi	90
面	miàn	229
哪	nǎ	49
南	nán	227
便	biàn/pián	204
前	qián	187
亲	qīn	110
甚	shén	36
是	shì	24
说	shuō	95
思	sī	148
為	wèi	136
洗	xǐ	189
星	xīng	77
要	yào	130
怎	zěn	160

10

班	bān	192
都	dōu	98
饿	è	170
高	gāo	162
哥	gē	115
个	gè	120
候	hòu	80
级	jí	146
家	jiā	89
們	men	34
能	néng	210
起	qǐ	30
钱	qián	134
请	qǐng	21

热	rè	166
時	shí	79
晚	wǎn	70
样	yàng	161
這	zhè	47

11

得	de/deǐ	99
够	gòu	211
夠	gòu	211
國	guó	88
過	guò	102
將	jiāng	131
累	lèi	168
离	lí	233
您	nín	42
商	shāng	222
視	shì	180
現	xiàn	72
谢	xiè	32
銀	yín	199
做	zuò	141

12

場	chǎng	223
等	děng	81
飯	fàn	171
給	gěi	212
貴	guì	203
黑	hēi	195
幾	jǐ	51
開	kāi	217

裡	lǐ	123
買	mǎi	201
期	qī	78
喜	xǐ	93
着	zháo	164
著	zháo	164
週	zhōu	175

13

飽	bǎo	172
當	dāng	140
道	dào	139
電	diàn	180
跟	gēn	207
號	hào	52
話	huà	96
會	huì	97
貨	huò	221
路	lù	225
嗎	ma	20
媽	mā	111
歲	suì	57
想	xiǎng	129
意	yì	147

14

對	duì	28
麼	me	37
睡	shuì	177
說	shuō	95
網	wǎng	184
銀	yín	199

| 遠 | yòng | 232 |
| 賺 | zhuàn | 133 |

15

餓	è	170
賣	mài	202
請	qǐng	21
熱	rè	166
樣	yàng	161
影	yǐng	182

16

錢	qián	134
親	qīn	110
興	xìng	163

17

幫	bāng	137
點	diǎn	76
還	hái	128
謝	xiè	32
賺	zhuàn	133

19

| 邊 | biān | 230 |
| 離 | lí | 233 |

20

| 覺 | jiào/jué | 178 |

22

| 歡 | huān | 94 |

Index III: Comparison of Traditional and Simplified Characters

Unit 1

們/们	嗎/吗	麼/么	請/请	謝/谢	見/见	對/对
men	ma	me	qǐng	xiè	jiàn	duì

Unit 2

幾/几	歲/岁	號/号	兒/儿	這/这
jǐ	suì	hào	ér	zhè

Unit 3

現/现	點/点	時/时
xiàn	diǎn	shí

Unit 4

國/国	會/会	説/说	話/话	過/过	歡/欢
guó	huì	shuō	huà	guò	huān

Unit 5

裡/里	個/个	媽/妈	親/亲	兩/两
lǐ	gè	mā	qīn	liǎng

Unit 6

將/将	來/来	級/级	為/为	當/当	賺/赚	錢/钱	幫/帮	還/还
jiāng	lái	jí	wèi	dāng	zhuàn	qián	bāng	hái

Unit 7

熱/热	餓/饿	飽/饱	樣/样	飯/饭	東/东	興/兴	著/着
rè	è	bǎo	yàng	fàn	dōng	xìng	zháo

Unit 8

電/电	視/视	網/网	覺/觉	週/周	後/后	門/门
diàn	shì	wǎng	jiào	zhōu	hòu	mén

Unit 9

買/买	賣/卖	紅/红	銀/银	貴/贵	夠/够	給/给
mǎi	mài	hóng	yín	guì	gòu	gěi

Unit 10

貨/货	場/场	離/离	遠/远	邊/边	開/开	車/车
huò	chǎng	lí	yòng	biān	kāi	chē

Some Useful References

Oxford Starter Chinese Dictionary (Oxford University Press, 2000). A very useful dictionary for the beginner in Chinese.

Fundamentals of Chinese Characters, by John Jing-hua Yin (Yale University Press, 2006). A great reference for instruction on recognizing and writing Chinese characters.

Speaking of Chinese, by Raymond Chang and Margaret Seogin Chang (Norton Publishing, 2001). A lively, inspired, and entertaining history of the Chinese language.

How to Be a More Successful Language Learner, by Joan Rubin and Irene Thompson (Heinle and Heinle Publishers, 1994). A great introduction to the strategies and tactics of language learning. A must read before and during your study.

China (Lonely Planet Publications). The best guide to China. Get the latest edition. A must take-along on your trip.

Chinese Characters: A Genealogy and Dictionary, by Rick Harbaugh (Yale University Press, 1998). Very, very useful on origins of characters with a fun website as well: Zhongwen.com.

Name:_____ Class:_____

Name:_____ **Class:**_____

Name:_____ **Class:**_____